The Empowered Student

A Guide to Self-Regulated Learning

NANCY WEINSTEIN

MARY-VICKI ALGERI

Copyright © 2018 by CAST, Inc.

All rights reserved. No part of this publication may be reproduced or transmitted in any form or by any means, electronic or mechanical, including photocopy, recording, or any information storage and retrieval systems, without permission in writing from the publisher.

Library of Congress Control Number: 2018939089

Paperback ISBN 978-1-930583-32-0
Ebook ISBN: 978-1-930583-33-7

Published by:
CAST Professional Publishing
an imprint of CAST, Inc.
Wakefield, Massachusetts, USA

For information about special discounts for bulk purchases, please email publishing@cast.org or telephone 781-245-2212 or visit www.castpublishing.org

Edited by Sue Miller Wiltz
Copyedited by Elizabeth Welch
Cover and interior design by Happenstance Type-O-Rama
Illustrations by Abby Weinstein except where otherwise noted. Illustrations for The Science of Learning (Figure 3) by Madeline Weinstein.

Special thanks to Dr. Wendy Matthews and Dr. Carol Blum: Without their expertise, teaching and guidance, this workbook would not have been possible.

Printed in the United States of America

Table of Contents

Introduction xi
How to Use This Workbook xxvii
Connections to Additional Frameworks and Standards xxix

Part 1: Foundation for Self-Regulated Learning

Lesson 1: The Science of Learning. 3

Lesson 2: The Importance of Mindset 9

Lesson 3: Nurturing a Growth Mindset. 19

Lesson 4: Intrinsic Motivation 25

Lesson 5: Developing Self-Awareness 33

Lesson 6: Understanding Strengths and Needs 45

Lesson 7: Academic Skills. 59

Lesson 8: Nonacademic Skills: Personal 67

Lesson 9: Nonacademic Skills: Cognitive 75

Part 2: Three-Step Process to Self-Regulated Learning

Lesson 10: Plan & Set Goals 99

Lesson 11: Try & Use Strategies. 111

Lesson 12: Reflect & Adapt 123

Conclusion 135
References 137

About the Authors

NANCY WEINSTEIN is the co-founder and CEO of Princeton, NJ–based Mindprint Learning. Starting in 2013, Mindprint has worked with schools, tutors, and educational consultants to help thousands of students better understand their learning needs and what they can do differently to succeed in school and in life. Nancy has a BSE in bioengineering from the University of Pennsylvania and an MBA from Harvard Business School. Prior to founding Mindprint, Nancy worked at a diverse group of companies, including Goldman Sachs, the Walt Disney Company, idealab!, and Bristol-Myers Squibb.

MARY-VICKI ALGERI is the Director of Learning at Mindprint Learning. She has a master's in early childhood education/special education from Teachers College and a bachelor's from Bowdoin College. Before joining Mindprint, she taught in both general and special education in elementary and middle school. She also provided consulting and curriculum development services to schools in New York and New Jersey.

About Mindprint Learning

Mindprint offers online solutions for schools, classrooms, tutoring centers, clinicians, and parents to support students' academic, social, and emotional development through a deeper understanding of their strengths and needs.

The Mindprint solution is designed to meet every child's unique learning needs with the Mindprint Assessment, Learner Profile, and Personalized Toolbox. The Mindprint Assessment was developed by neuroscientists at the University of Pennsylvania's Perelman School of Medicine in collaboration with the National Institutes of Mental Health (NIMH) (Moore, Reise, Gur, Hakonarson, & Gur, 2015). The Assessment was normed on more than 10,000 children and has been referenced in 250-plus peer-reviewed journal articles. You can be confident that you are giving your students an accurate and reliable indicator of their cognitive strengths and needs. The results are presented in the Learner Profile, a detailed explanation of each student's complex reasoning, executive functions, and memory and speed skills, with personalized learning recommendations from our educational experts. With the recommendations and the Personalized Toolbox, you will have the learning strategies and solutions you need to support every student across academic subjects. Use the promo code CAST25 to get 25% off the website subscription price. Please contact us directly about school and classroom discounts.

Mindprint's solution can be used for general screening of learning differences, and giftedness. It is also at the core of many schools' personalized learning solutions, classroom and one-on-one instruction, social-emotional learning curricula, and advisory programs.

Find out more about Mindprint Learning here: *https://mindprintlearning.com/faqs/*

A Note from Mindprint's Founder

It's a dream come true to have this workbook published by CAST. Admittedly, it's not the dream I would have anticipated six years ago given my not-so-straightforward path to get here. However, I'm glad to play even the smallest role in helping you guide your students to their full potential. Although that might sound like a lofty goal, the research is clear that self-regulated learning is one of the most important skills you can impart to your students.

Before diving in, you deserve to know that I was trained to be an engineer—not an educator. My journey into the field of education began later in life, only after choosing to be a stay-at-home mom with two elementary school daughters. As an engineer, when I see a problem I assume a solution is readily available. Or at least, it's my job to find one.

However, as most parents quickly do, I discovered that not all of life's challenges are easily fixable. Nothing was wrong with my kids per se. But it would be fair to say that nothing with my older daughter was ever simple—not eating, not sleeping, not anything. My husband and I couldn't pinpoint anything specific, and there's really no one to help with "nothing is ever easy."

The challenges with Abby's complexities peaked in third grade. Her wonderful, experienced, and very thoughtful teacher explained that "more data" would help her unlock Abby's full potential. It took several more conversations to understand that "more data" was teacher code for cognitive testing. We learned that since cognitive testing is very expensive and time consuming, most teachers feel uncomfortable recommending testing for students unless they suspect a learning difference.

I asked the child psychologist what I should tell Abby about the testing. It was going to be a lot of hours outside of school, and my very inquisitive child was sure to demand an explanation. The response was simple: "You tell her you are giving her a gift. The gift of how she learns. It is a gift she will take with her the rest of her life."

Fast-forward six years, and Abby is a happy, successful high school student whose potential definitely has been "unlocked." In those years I've spoken with hundreds of parents who have shared their painful stories of coded conversations about bright but struggling students. I'm thrilled Mindprint can share the gift of how a student learns—at a fraction of the time and expense—so that the potential of every student can be unlocked with fewer struggles.

The Mindprint Assessment takes only one hour on any computer with no special expertise required. Although we charge for the Assessment, we've done our best to keep it as affordable as possible.

Self-awareness is a gift, but it is still grossly insufficient. My interactions with researchers, educators, and parents around the world, including the wonderful team at CAST, taught me that understanding is only helpful if you know how to act on it. My own experience confirmed the research. I quickly learned that if Abby wasn't a willing participant, it wasn't going to be a particularly useful gift at all.

With this knowledge and scientific evidence as our guide, we went one step further in developing Mindprint. We created what we call a Personalized Toolbox of learning strategies—in other words, learning techniques based on scientific evidence of how the brain understands, retains, and processes information. Just as each student's Learner Profile is different, so are the strategies he or she will need to be a successful learner.

Every educator, parent, and student can use the Toolbox of 500-plus evidence-based strategies for free, even if your students don't have Learner Profiles. Each strategy is written so it is clear who it works best for, in which situations, and why. Just anticipate that you will need to help your students make good choices, listen to what they say works and doesn't work, and adapt accordingly. In short, students can achieve self-regulated learning success without Learner Profiles but they should anticipate a bit more trial-and-error in the process.

The three categories of strategies are as follows:

- Instructional strategies intended for all teachers to use in their classrooms of diverse learners

- Parenting strategies intended for parents to support students at home

- Study strategies written for students to teach them how to work independently and efficiently

I want to emphasize the importance of students being onboard with the process. If your students aren't yet convinced that it's their responsibility to learn, it will be challenging for them to be successful.

Part 1 of this book is dedicated to getting students onboard. It lays the foundation for self-regulated learning and includes lessons on the basic neuroscience on how learning happens and what that means in practical terms for effort and motivation. We include lessons on the seminal growth-mindset work of Stanford professor Carol Dweck, recognizing that students who do not fundamentally believe they are capable of learning and growing—regardless of the advantages, threats, and distractions from their external environment—are unlikely to reach their full potential (Dweck, 2016).

With that core foundation in place, Part 2 gets specific. We delve into exactly what self-regulated learning looks like in the classroom. Here, we rely on the overarching framework for processing and implementation developed by David Rose and the researchers at CAST (Meyer, Rose, & Gordon, 2014). We lead you through the self-regulated learning process of planning and goal setting, trying and using strategies, and reflecting and adapting (Panadero, 2017).

We are light on words in this workbook and heavy on examples. Keep in mind that self-regulation is not a skill, like long division, that educators teach and students master. Rather, it is a way of being. Developing self-regulation requires patient, caring adults who expect an iterative process and anticipate student mistakes as part of the learning and growing process. Adults must recognize that kids will continue to need sustained support and encouragement throughout adolescence. Neuroscientific evidence is clear that only in early adulthood can we expect students will finally have the combined physical, mental, and emotional capacity to self-regulate on their own (Center on the Developing Child, Harvard University, 2012). Of course, some students will need more support than others on this journey.

We hope you use the ideas and examples in this book, but also enhance them or try new activities of your own. We want the activities to be relevant, valuable, and authentic to the diverse learners in your classroom and help them to celebrate their unique strengths, accept their imperfections, and know when and how to ask for help.

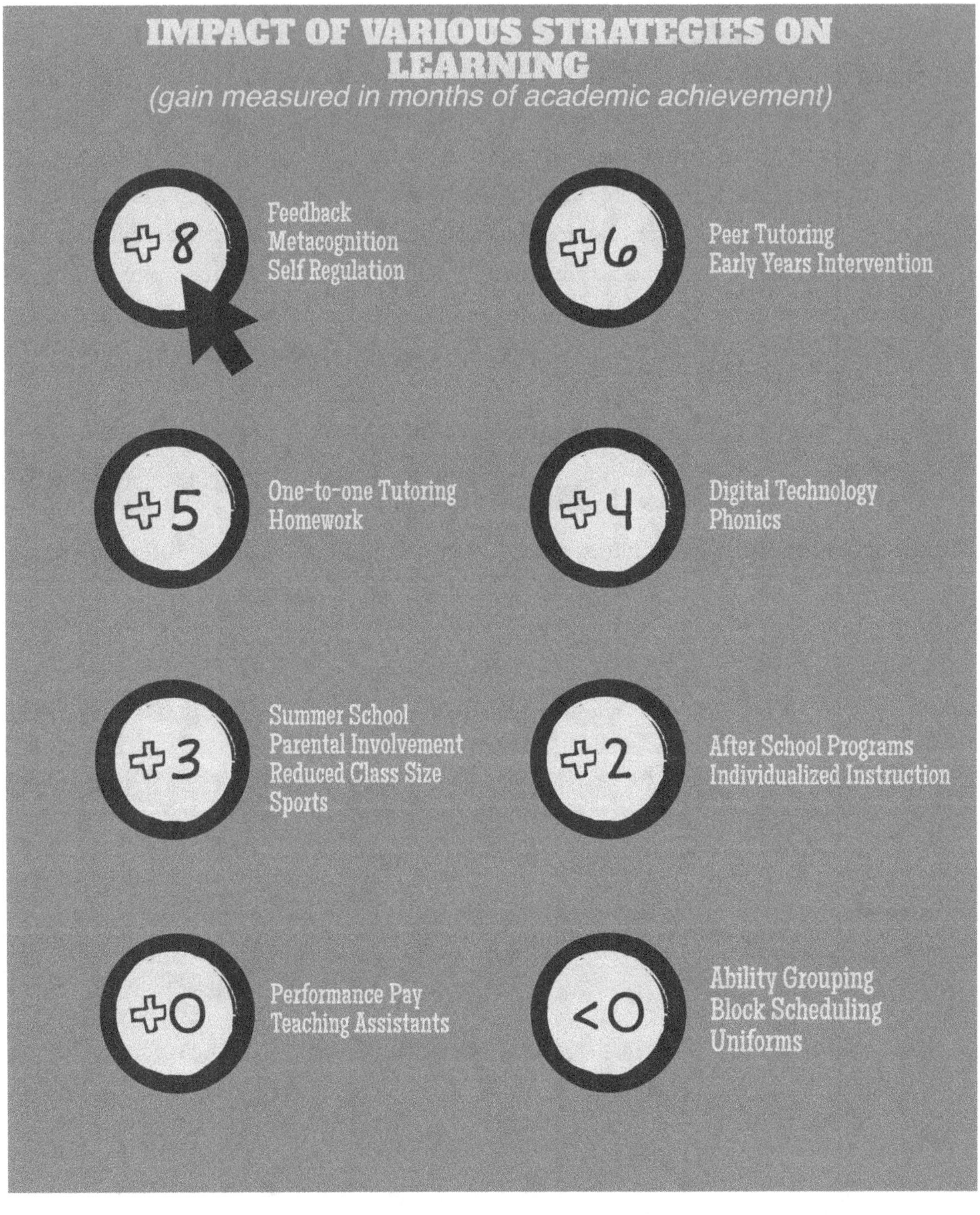

IMPACT OF VARIOUS STRATEGIES ON LEARNING
(gain measured in months of academic achievement)

- **+8** Feedback, Metacognition, Self Regulation
- **+6** Peer Tutoring, Early Years Intervention
- **+5** One-to-one Tutoring, Homework
- **+4** Digital Technology, Phonics
- **+3** Summer School, Parental Involvement, Reduced Class Size, Sports
- **+2** After School Programs, Individualized Instruction
- **+0** Performance Pay, Teaching Assistants
- **<0** Ability Grouping, Block Scheduling, Uniforms

Figure 1: Impact of various strategies on learning
Source: Higgins, Kokotsaki, & Coe, 2012

Introduction

What Is Self-Regulated Learning?

Self-regulated learning is a process by which students direct and monitor their own learning (Zimmerman & Schunk, 1989). The process includes students identifying how they learn best and taking responsibility for their learning progress. Students start to become self-regulated learners by understanding the neuroscience of how learning happens. Then they are most open to understanding and accepting their own capabilities and needs, using strategies to learn effectively, and possessing the mindset and motivation to keep growing and improving.

Why Is Self-Regulated Learning Important?

We know that when students take responsibility for their own learning, they are more intrinsically motivated, leading to a virtuous cycle of continuous effort and improvement. The UK-based Education Endowment Foundation evaluated the impact of high potential strategies on learning. Based on a meta study that included over 10,000 independent research studies, the EEF found that feedback, metacognition and self-regulation delivered greater impact, as measured in months of academic achievement, than other strategies, including one-to-one tutoring, reduced class size, and extended school days (Higgins, Kokotsaki, & Coe, 2012).

The reason self-regulated learning is so effective is that it has universal applicability, regardless of ability or past achievement. Unlike strategies such as spaced repetition for students with weaker memories or manipulatives for students needing more hands-on representations, self-regulation is equally important for all students. All students have relative strengths and needs, and all students benefit from taking feedback and learning how to improve, regardless of their starting point.

Self-regulated learning also addresses a more practical constraint. Although teachers should provide students with choices (see the great resources of CAST), they need to feel confident that students are able to make good choices that will serve them well. In addition, all the achievement data in the world cannot accurately inform a teacher about who wants to learn more, who understands but cannot focus, and who could learn if the material were just presented in a different way. Teachers need students to inform them.

This workbook is intended for educators to nurture self-awareness and metacognition in their students so that students have a desire to learn, understand what they need to succeed, and are comfortable speaking up when they need guidance and help.

How Does Self-Regulated Learning Align with Universal Design for Learning (UDL) Principles?

Readers of this workbook who are also students of UDL might notice that the overarching goal of self-regulated learning is strikingly consistent with the goal of applying UDL to instruction: "help all learners to develop into expert learners…who can assess their own learning needs, monitor their own progress, and regulate and sustain their interests, effort, and persistence during learning tasks" (CAST, 2012).

For readers who will use this workbook in the context of their broader UDL implementation, we provide the following "crosswalk" to enable you to clearly visualize how the specific lessons and activities in this workbook align to UDL Guidelines and will support you in achieving your UDL goals. Read more about the UDL Guidelines here: *udlguidelines.cast.org* (CAST, 2018).

UDL GUIDELINE	MINDPRINT LESSON	MINDPRINT ACTIVITY
Promote expectations and beliefs that optimize motivation	Lesson 1: The Science of Learning	Building My Brain Class Brain
	Lesson 2: The Importance of Mindset	What Is Growth Mindset? Sharing & Storytelling I Can Help Myself Grow Everyone Makes Mistakes I Can Be Famous Ted Talk: Write Your Story, Change History, by Brad Meltzer
	Lesson 3: Nurturing a Growth Mindset	Ted Talk by Harry Potter author J. K. Rowling Speaking Growth Mindset Classroom Culture Celebrate Risk

UDL GUIDELINE	MINDPRINT LESSON	MINDPRINT ACTIVITY
Promote expectations and beliefs that optimize motivation *(continued)*	Lesson 4: Intrinsic Motivation	Motivation Classroom Rules and Commandments Choice Assignments
	Lesson 5: Developing Self-Awareness	Dialogue Journal
	Lesson 6: Understanding Strengths & Needs	Sweet Spot of Learning Success WEF Career Skills (I & II)
	Lesson 7: Academic Skills	Academic Skills and Learning Academic Skills Beyond Grades
	Lesson 8: Nonacademic Skills: Personal	Understanding Personal Skills Throw Away Test Anxiety
	Lesson 9: Nonacademic Skills: Cognitive	How I Use My… Cognitive Skills Prioritization
	Lesson 11: Try & Use Strategies	What Are Strategies? Strategy Selection Developing Metacognition I Haven't Yet
Facilitate personal coping skills and strategies	Lesson 2: The Importance of Mindset	What Is Growth Mindset? Sharing & Storytelling I Can Help Myself Grow Everyone Makes Mistakes I Can Be Famous Ted Talk: Write Your Story, Change History, by Brad Meltzer
	Lesson 3: Nurturing a Growth Mindset	Ted Talk by Harry Potter author J. K. Rowling Project-Based Learning Speaking Growth Mindset Classroom Culture Celebrate Risk
	Lesson 4: Intrinsic Motivation	Classroom Rules and Commandments

UDL GUIDELINE	MINDPRINT LESSON	MINDPRINT ACTIVITY
Facilitate personal coping skills and strategies *(continued)*	Lesson 5: Developing Self-Awareness	What Is Metacognition? This Is What I'm Thinking Dialogue Journal Metacognition Questions
	Lesson 6: Understanding Strengths & Needs	Sweet Spot of Learning Success
	Lesson 7: Academic Skills	Study Schedule
	Lesson 8: Nonacademic Skills: Personal	Understanding Personal Skills Throw Away Test Anxiety Collaboration Skills Group Reflection Mental Health Breaks Student Groupings
	Lesson 9: Nonacademic Skills: Cognitive	Personalized Learning Plan How I Use My… Cognitive Skills Prioritization
	Lesson 10: Plan & Set Goals	Goal Setting Goals We Can Measure Individual Goal Setting Make Goals Visible
	Lesson 11: Try & Use Strategies	What Are Strategies? Strategy Selection Developing Metacognition Strategy Action Plan I Haven't Yet Create a Contingency Plan Assignment Wrappers
	Lesson 12: Reflect & Adapt	Let's Talk About Reflection Assignment Wrappers Interim Reflection Daily Reflection
Develop self-assessment and reflection	Lesson 2: The Importance of Mindset	Sharing & Storytelling I Can Help Myself Grow Everyone Makes Mistakes I Can Be Famous Ted Talk: Write Your Story, Change History, by Brad Meltzer

UDL GUIDELINE	MINDPRINT LESSON	MINDPRINT ACTIVITY
Develop self-assessment and reflection *(continued)*	Lesson 3: Nurturing a Growth Mindset	Project-Based Learning Speaking Growth Mindset Classroom Culture Celebrate Risk
	Lesson 4: Intrinsic Motivation	Motivation Hackschooling Makes Me Happy My Interests and Passions
	Lesson 5: Developing Self-Awareness	What Is Metacognition? This Is What I'm Thinking Dialogue Journal Exit Slip Metacognition Questions
	Lesson 6: Understanding Strengths and Needs	Sweet Spot of Learning Success WEF Career Skills (I & II) This Is Me
	Lesson 7: Academic Skills	Academic Skills and Learning Academic Skills Beyond Grades Study Schedule
	Lesson 8: Nonacademic Skills: Personal	Understanding Personal Skills Throw Away Test Anxiety Collaboration Skills Group Reflection Mental Health Breaks
	Lesson 9: Nonacademic Skills: Cognitive	Personalized Learning Plan How I Use My… Cognitive Skills Prioritization
	Lesson 11: Try & Use Strategies	Strategy Selection Developing Metacognition Strategy Action Plan I Haven't Yet Create a Contingency Plan Assignment Wrapper
	Lesson 12: Reflect & Adapt	Let's Talk About Reflection Interim Reflection Track Progress Daily Reflection/Model Reflection

UDL GUIDELINE	MINDPRINT LESSON	MINDPRINT ACTIVITY
Heighten salience of goals and objectives	Lesson 2: The Importance of Mindset	Everyone Makes Mistakes I Can Be Famous Ted Talk: Write Your Story, Change History, by Brad Meltzer
	Lesson 3: Nurturing a Growth Mindset	Ted Talk by Harry Potter author J. K. Rowling Project-Based Learning Speaking Growth Mindset
	Lesson 6: Understanding Strengths & Needs	WEF Career Skills (I & II)
	Lesson 7: Academic Skills	Study Schedule
	Lesson 9: Nonacademic Skills: Cognitive	Personalized Learning Plan
	Lesson 10: Plan & Set Goals	Goal Setting Goals We Can Measure Individual Goal Setting
	Lesson 11: Try & Use Strategies	Strategy Action Plan I Haven't Yet Create a Contingency Plan Assignment Wrapper
	Lesson 12: Reflect & Adapt	Let's Talk About Reflection Interim Reflection

UDL GUIDELINE	MINDPRINT LESSON	MINDPRINT ACTIVITY
Vary demands and resources to optimize challenge	Lesson 8: Nonacademic Skills: Personal	Student Groupings
	Lesson 9: Nonacademic Skills: Cognitive	Personalized Learning Plan
	Lesson 10: Plan & Set Goals	Goal Setting Goals We Can Measure Individual Goal Setting Make Goals Visible
	Lesson 11: Try & Use Strategies	Developing Metacognition Strategy Action Plan I Haven't Yet Assignment Wrapper
Foster collaboration and community	Lesson 1: The Science of Learning	Class Brain
	Lesson 2: The Importance of Mindset	Sharing & Storytelling I Can Help Myself Grow
	Lesson 3: Nurturing a Growth Mindset	Classroom Culture
	Lesson 4: Intrinsic Motivation	Classroom Rules and Commandments
	Lesson 5: Developing Self-Awareness	Dialogue Journal
	Lesson 6: Understanding Strengths & Needs	WEF Career Skills (II)
	Lesson 8: Nonacademic Skills: Personal	Understanding Personal Skills Collaboration Skills Group Reflection Student Groupings

UDL GUIDELINE	MINDPRINT LESSON	MINDPRINT ACTIVITY
Increase mastery-oriented feedback	Lesson 1: The Science of Learning	Class Brain
	Lesson 2: Importance of Mindset	I Can Be Famous Ted Talk: Write Your Story, Change History, by Brad Meltzer
	Lesson 3: Nurturing a Growth Mindset	Project-Based Learning Speaking Growth Mindset Classroom Culture Celebrate Risk
	Lesson 4: Intrinsic Motivation	Hackschooling Makes Me Happy
	Lesson 5: Developing Self-Awareness	Dialogue Journal
	Lesson 8: Nonacademic Skills: Personal	Group Reflection
	Lesson 9: Nonacademic Skills: Cognitive	Cognitive Skills Prioritization
	Lesson 12: Reflect & Adapt	Interim Reflection

UDL GUIDELINE	MINDPRINT LESSON	MINDPRINT ACTIVITY
Optimize individual choice and autonomy	Lesson 2: The Importance of Mindset	I Can Be Famous Ted Talk: Write Your Story, Change History, by Brad Meltzer
	Lesson 3: Nurturing a Growth Mindset	Project-Based Learning Speaking Growth Mindset Classroom Culture Celebrate Risk
	Lesson 4: Intrinsic Motivation	Motivation Hackschooling Makes Me Happy Choice Assignments
	Lesson 5: Developing Self-Awareness	This Is What I'm Thinking Dialogue Journal
	Lesson 6: Understanding Strengths & Needs	Sweet Spot of Learning Success
	Lesson 9: Nonacademic Skills: Cognitive	Personalized Learning Plan Cognitive Skills Prioritization
	Lesson 10: Plan & Set Goals	Goal Setting Goals We Can Measure Individual Goal Setting
	Lesson 11: Try & Use Strategies	Strategy Selection Developing Metacognition Strategy Action Plan I Haven't Yet Create a Contingency Plan Assignment Wrapper
	Lesson 12: Reflect & Adapt	Let's Talk About Reflection Interim Reflection

UDL GUIDELINE	MINDPRINT LESSON	MINDPRINT ACTIVITY
Optimize relevance, value and authenticity	Lesson 1: The Science of Learning	Teach with Science of Learning Infographic Building My Brain Class Brain
	Lesson 2: The Importance of Mindset	Sharing & Storytelling Everyone Makes Mistakes I Can Be Famous Ted Talk: Write Your Story, Change History, by Brad Meltzer
	Lesson 3: Nurturing a Growth Mindset	Ted Talk by Harry Potter author J. K. Rowling Project-Based Learning Speaking Growth Mindset Classroom Culture Grade-Free Assignments Celebrate Risk
	Lesson 4: Intrinsic Motivation	Motivation Hackschooling Makes Me Happy My Interests and Passions Choice Assignments
	Lesson 6: Understanding Strengths & Needs	Sweet Spot of Learning Success WEF Career Skills (Parts I & II)
	Lesson 7: Academic Skills	Academic Skills Beyond Grades
	Lesson 9: Nonacademic Skills: Cognitive	Personalized Learning Plan How I Use My... Cognitive Skills Prioritization
	Lesson 10: Plan & Set Goals	Goal Setting Goals We Can Measure Individual Goal Setting Make Goals Visible
	Lesson 11: Try & Use Strategies	I Haven't Yet

UDL GUIDELINE	MINDPRINT LESSON	MINDPRINT ACTIVITY
Minimize threats and distractions	Lesson 2: The Importance of Mindset	Sharing & Storytelling I Can Help Myself Grow Everyone Makes Mistakes
	Lesson 3: Nurturing a Growth Mindset	Ted Talk by Harry Potter author J. K. Rowling Speaking Growth Mindset Classroom Culture Grade-Free Assignments
	Lesson 4: Intrinsic Motivation	Classroom Rules and Commandments
	Lesson 5: Developing Self-Awareness	What Is Metacognition? This Is What I'm Thinking Dialogue Journal Exit Slip Metacognition Questions
	Lesson 7: Academic Skills	Academic Skills and Learning Academic Skills Beyond Grades
	Lesson 8: Nonacademic Skills: Personal	Understanding Personal Skills Throw Away Test Anxiety Collaboration Skills Mental Health Breaks Student Groupings
	Lesson 9: Nonacademic Skills: Cognitive	Personalized Learning Plan Cognitive Skills Prioritization
	Lesson 11: Try & Use Strategies	What Are Strategies? Strategy Selection Developing Metacognition Strategy Action Plan I Haven't Yet Create a Contingency Plan Assignment Wrapper
	Lesson 12: Reflect & Adapt	Interim Reflection

UDL Principle: Provide multiple means of representation to develop resourceful, knowledgeable learners

UDL GUIDELINE	MINDPRINT LESSON	MINDPRINT ACTIVITY
Provide options for comprehension ▸ Activate or supply background knowledge ▸ Highlight patterns, critical features, big ideas, and relationships ▸ Guide information processing, visualization, and manipulation ▸ Maximize transfer and generalization	Lesson 3: Nurturing a Growth Mindset Lesson 7: Academic Skills Lesson 11: Try & Use Strategies	Classroom Culture Academic Skills and Learning Use a New Strategy Interleaving What Are Strategies? Strategy Selection Developing Metacognition Strategy Action Plan Assignment Wrapper
Provide options for language, mathematical expressions, and symbols ▸ Illustrate through multiple media	Lesson 7: Academic Skills Lesson 11: Try & Use Strategies	Use a New Strategy What Are Strategies? Strategy Selection Developing Metacognition Strategy Action Plan Assignment Wrapper
Provide options for perception ▸ Offer ways of customizing the display of information ▸ Offer alternatives for auditory/visual information	Lesson 7: Academic Skills Lesson 10: Plan & Set Goals Lesson 11: Try & Use Strategies	Use a New Strategy Make Goals Visible What Are Strategies? Strategy Selection Developing Metacognition Strategy Action Plan Assignment Wrapper

UDL Principle: Provide multiple means of action & expression to develop strategic, goal-directed learners

UDL GUIDELINE	MINDPRINT LESSON	MINDPRINT ACTIVITY
Guide appropriate goal-setting	Lesson 3: Nurturing a Growth Mindset	Project-Based Learning Classroom Culture
	Lesson 5: Developing Self-Awareness	What Is Metacognition? Dialogue Journal
	Lesson 6: Understanding Strengths & Needs	WEF Career Skills (I & II)
	Lesson 7: Academic Skills	Academic Skills Beyond Grades Study Schedule
	Lesson 8: Nonacademic Skills: Personal	Understanding Personal Skills
	Lesson 9: Nonacademic Skills: Cognitive	Personalized Learning Plan Cognitive Skills Prioritization
	Lesson 10: Plan & Set Goals	Goal Setting Goals We Can Measure Individual Goal Setting Make Goals Visible
	Lesson 11: Try & Use Strategies	Developing Metacognition I Haven't Yet

UDL Principle: Provide multiple means of action & expression to develop strategic, goal-directed learners *(continued)*

UDL GUIDELINE	MINDPRINT LESSON	MINDPRINT ACTIVITY
Support planning and strategy development	Lesson 3: Nurturing a Growth Mindset	Project-Based Learning Speaking Growth Mindset Classroom Culture
	Lesson 5: Developing Self-Awareness	Dialogue Journal
	Lesson 6: Understanding Strengths & Needs	WEF Career Skills (I & II)
	Lesson 7: Academic Skills	Study Schedule Use a New Strategy
	Lesson 8: Nonacademic Skills: Personal	Understanding Personal Skills
	Lesson 9: Nonacademic Skills: Cognitive	Personalized Learning Plan How I Use My... Cognitive Skills Prioritization
	Lesson 10: Plan & Set Goals	Goal Setting Goals We Can Measure Individual Goal Setting Make Goals Visible
	Lesson 11: Try & Use Strategies	What Are Strategies? Strategy Selection Developing Metacognition Strategy Action Plan Create a Contingency Plan Assignment Wrapper
	Lesson 12: Reflect & Adapt	Interim Reflection

UDL Principle: Provide multiple means of action & expression to develop strategic, goal-directed learners *(continued)*

UDL GUIDELINE	MINDPRINT LESSON	MINDPRINT ACTIVITY
Enhance capacity for monitoring progress	Lesson 1: The Science of Learning	Class Brain
	Lesson 2: The Importance of Mindset	I Can Help Myself Grow Everyone Makes Mistakes
	Lesson 3: Nurturing a Growth Mindset	Project-Based Learning Speaking Growth Mindset Classroom Culture Celebrate Risk
	Lesson 5: Developing Self-Awareness	What Is Metacognition? This Is What I'm Thinking Dialogue Journal Exit Slip Metacognition Questions
	Lesson 6: Understanding Strengths & Needs	Sweet Spot of Learning Success
	Lesson 7: Academic Skills	Study Schedule Interleaving
	Lesson 8: Nonacademic Skills: Personal	Collaboration Skills Group Reflection Mental Health Breaks
	Lesson 9: Nonacademic Skills: Cognitive:	Personalized Learning Plan How I Use My… Cognitive Skills Prioritization
	Lesson 10: Plan & Set Goals	Make Goals Visible
	Lesson 11: Try & Use Strategies	Developing Metacognition Strategy Action Plan Assignment Wrapper
	Lesson 12: Reflect & Adapt	Let's Talk About Reflection Interim Reflection

UDL Principle: Provide multiple means of action & expression to develop strategic, goal-directed learners *(continued)*

UDL GUIDELINE	MINDPRINT LESSON	MINDPRINT ACTIVITY
Use multiple media for communication	Lesson 5: Developing Self-Awareness	Show Your Thinking
	Lesson 10: Plan & Set Goals	Make Goals Visible
	Lesson 11: Try & Use Strategies	What Are Strategies? Strategy Selection Strategy Action Plan
Use multiple tools for construction and composition	Lesson 11: Try & Use Strategies	What Are Strategies? Strategy Selection Strategy Action Plan
Build fluencies with graduated levels of support for practice and performance	Lesson 3: Nurturing a Growth Mindset	Project-Based Learning Classroom Culture Speaking Growth Mindset Celebrate Risk
	Lesson 7: Academic Skills	Academic Skills and Learning Use a New Strategy Interleaving
	Lesson 9: Nonacademic Skills: Cognitive	Personalized Learning Plan
	Lesson 11: Try & Use Strategies	Create a Contingency Plan Assignment Wrapper
Vary the methods of response and navigation	Lesson 11: Try & Use Strategies	What Are Strategies? Strategy Selection Strategy Action Plan Create a Contingency Plan
Optimize access to tools and assistive technologies	Lesson 7: Academic Skills	Use a New Strategy
	Lesson 9: Nonacademic Skills: Cognitive	Personalized Learning Plan

How to Use This Workbook

Through a series of mini-lessons that can supplement your existing curriculum, this workbook will help you develop the skills students need to implement self-regulated learning. Each lesson is designed to focus more on student voice and choice rather than pedagogy. In each chapter, you will find explanations of key concepts, teaching guidance, options for activities, and visual aids.

Vital Vocab

These are the key vocabulary terms students should learn in the lesson. A more comprehensive online glossary of terms to support self-regulated learning can be found on the Mindprint Learning website (*https://mindprintlearning.com/free-resources/glossary-of-terms/*).

Teacher Takeaways

Key points every teacher wants to consider before introducing the concepts and lessons to students.

Student Takeaways

Each lesson has up to three key take-home points for students.

Mindprint Strategies for Students

These are learning strategies associated with the lesson concepts. In contrast to Lesson 11's Try & Use Strategies, which should be chosen by the student, these strategies are chosen by the teacher to use for the lesson. Some of these strategies are teacher-led or instructional (T). Others are student-led (S). We highly recommend printing them out or, if your students have Personalized Toolboxes, adding them to their online Learning Plans so they can refer to them throughout the year.

A Closer Look

Dig deeper on each topic with these suggested resources.

Lesson Activities

Suggested activities and approaches for reinforcing lesson concepts. In addition to Student Activity worksheets included with each lesson, you can also find examples of completed worksheets available on the CAST Professional Publishing website (*http://castpublishing.org/books-media/empowered-student/resources/#how-to*). Each activity is followed by a combination of letters (E, M, H) to describe the most suitable audience. Anticipate that some activities will require modification based on the specific age group. E = Elementary, M = Middle Grades, H = High School

Direct Instruction

Suggestions for introducing concepts and teacher-led discussion.

Student Activity

Opportunities for students to gain hands-on experience with the lesson concepts. Activity sheets are provided in the lessons.

Coaching

Most of the concepts in this book require ongoing support and reinforcement. These are suggestions so teachers can continue to instill these concepts beyond the mini-lessons.

Connections to Additional Frameworks and Standards

You can certainly still use this workbook even if you have not adopted UDL. Self-regulation is essential for all students. The following are just a few of the many frameworks and standards that the chapters in this book will help you address. The concepts and intended outcomes of this guide provide the tools for you to reach the overarching goal of preparing students for subsequent school years, careers, and life as self-regulated learners.

- AMLE: This We Believe: The 16 Characteristics of Successful Schools (*www.amle.org/AboutAMLE/ThisWeBelieve/tabid/121/Default.aspx#122516-the-16-characteristics*)

- ASCA Mindsets & Behaviors for Student Success: K–12 College- and Career-Readiness Standards for Every Student (*http://schoolcounselor.org/asca/media/asca/home/MindsetsBehaviors.pdf*)

- Bloom's Taxonomy (*https://cft.vanderbilt.edu//cft/guides-sub-pages/blooms-taxonomy*)

- CASEL (*https://casel.org/core-competencies/*)

- Common Core State Standards (*www.corestandards.org/*)

- McREL International Online Standards Compendium (*www2.mcrel.org/compendium/*)

- Framework for 21st Century Learning (*www.p21.org/about-us/p21-framework*)

- 2016 ISTE (International Society for Technology in Education) Standards for Students (*http://www.iste.org/standards/for-students*)

PART 1

Foundation for Self-Regulated Learning

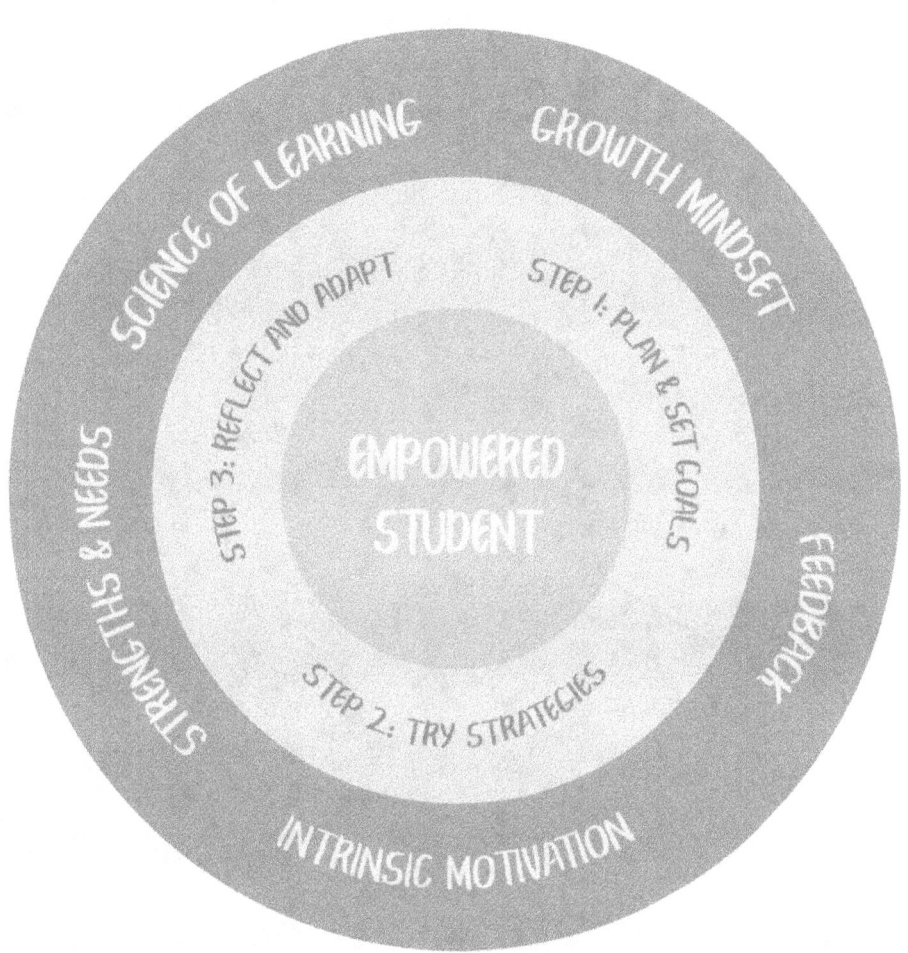

Figure 2: Self-regulated learning overview

Self-regulated learning is unlikely to be successful if students are unprepared or unwilling to rise to the challenge. Part 1 will help you cultivate the mindsets in your students that are a prerequisite for effective self-regulated learning: understanding the science of learning, developing and nurturing a growth mindset, cultivating intrinsic motivation, and becoming intimately familiar with your strengths and needs.

Figure 3: The science of learning

Lesson 1

The Science of Learning

Neuroscience proves that all students have great capacity for learning throughout their lifetimes. However, that does not mean we all learn the same way or start from the same place. Everyone has a different combination of learning strengths and needs, which means that some skills and learning will come more easily than others. For skills that come less easily, students can make progress with the right mindset. However, you can expect that they might need to practice more or try different approaches.

VITAL VOCAB

dopamine: A brain chemical that is released by positive emotions and strengthens synapses.

neurons: Another name for brain cells. The typical brain has about 100 billion neurons.

neuroplasticity: Scientific explanation of how the brain changes and develops over time based on practice, experience, and maturity. Neuroplasticity shows that although the brain is most malleable during early childhood, the brain continues to develop throughout adolescence and adulthood with practice and effort. In short, you can always grow, learn, and improve.

neuroscience: A branch of science specifically devoted to how the brain develops and acquires new information.

synapse: The connection between neurons. The number and strength of synapses determine depth of understanding and likelihood of recall. Synapses grow stronger with repeated exposure and practice.

TEACHER TAKEAWAYS

- When students understand the scientific evidence that practice and effort (not only genetics) determine how much you know, they are more likely to work harder because they believe they can succeed.

- A very basic overview of neuroplasticity, as provided in this section, is typically sufficient for students of all ages.

- Although basic neuroplasticity can be presented in a very brief lesson, it is important to reinforce these concepts consistently in daily language and with "teachable moment" opportunities.

- Understanding neuroplasticity can be equally important for high achievers and struggling learners:

  - High achievers need to understand that regardless of any innate talents they might possess, their continued success depends on hard work and effort.

  - Struggling learners should know that they are capable of learning but that sometimes they might need to work harder or try different approaches. They also might discover areas where they are ahead of their classmates and do not need to work as hard.

 ## STUDENT TAKEAWAYS

- The brain is like a muscle; it grows when exercised by strengthening synapses. You grow your brain through practice, taking on challenges, and a good attitude—all of which you can control.

- Everyone can learn if he or she works hard. Some skills will be easier and some will require more effort. Each person's "harder" and "easier" skills are different.

- If you don't practice, even if you learned easily, synapses will weaken and you might forget or not be able to apply the information when you need it. Everyone needs to practice and work hard.

MINDPRINT STRATEGIES FOR STUDENTS

- Growth Mindset Basics (*https://my.mindprintlearning.com/toolbox/toolbox-demo/product/11447*)(T, S)

- Helping the Perfectionist (*https://my.mindprintlearning.com/toolbox/toolbox-demo/product/12180*) (T)

- Handling Peer Interactions for Students with Learning Differences (*https://my.mindprintlearning.com/toolbox/toolbox-demo/product/11522*) (T)

A CLOSER LOOK

- Engaging Brains: How to Enhance Learning by Teaching Kids about Neuroplasticity; edutopia.org (*www.edutopia.org/blog/neuroplasticity-engage-brains-enhance-learning-donna-wilson*)

- You Can Learn Anything; Khan Academy (*www.khanacademy.org/youcanlearnanything*)

- 35 Strategies to Developing a Growth Mindset; Mindprint Learning (*mindprintlearning.com/blog/where-we-go-from-here/*)

LESSON ACTIVITIES

Direct Instruction

Discuss the Science of Learning infographic with an emphasis on the importance of effort and practice in growing your brain and reaching your learning goals. The CAST website (*http://castpublishing.org/books-media/empowered-student/resources/#lesson-1*) has cutouts to introduce this graphic in pieces. (E, M, H)

Student Activity

Building My Brain: Students write about a time when they worked hard and succeeded. (E, M, H)

Coaching

Hang the Science of Learning graphic in your room. When students remember something unexpected, you can comment, "Those synapses must be really strong." If they have difficulty, you can say, "I guess we just need to practice and strengthen those synapses. Good thing we have lots of brain cells to work with." Ongoing reinforcement of the science is important. (E, M, H)

Coaching

Class Brain: Create a "class brain" for the classroom wall. Whenever a student displays growth mindset, have him or her add a "synapse" to the picture. This could be a drawing, pins with string, etc. (E, M)

STUDENT ACTIVITY:
Building My Brain

Name: _____

Think of a time when you learned something very challenging. It could be a lesson in school, a sports skill, or a project you made at home.

Act out, draw a comic, make a poster, or write about what was happening in your brain as you were learning and mastering the skill. Be sure to discuss synapses and neurons in your presentation.

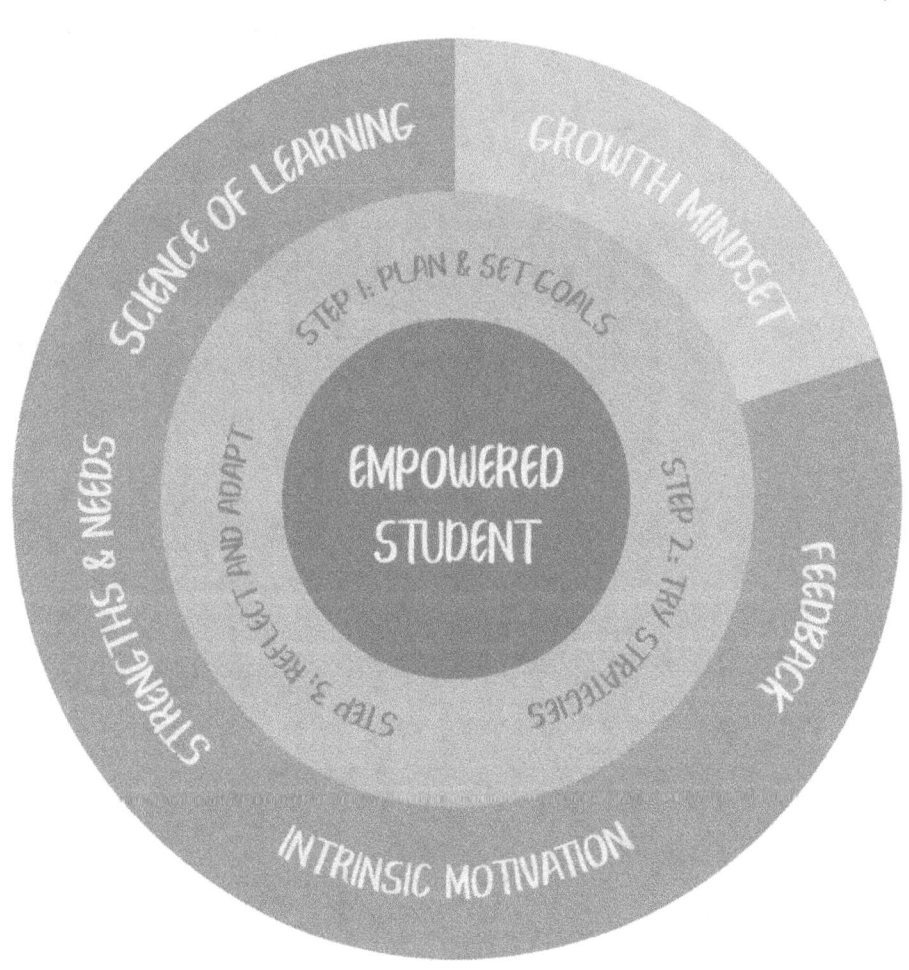

Figure 4: Growth mindset

Lesson 2

The Importance of Mindset

If students approach learning with a growth mindset, they believe they're in control of improving their performance and achieving their goals. Over time, this leads to improved self-confidence and a resilience that helps them continue to strive and grow even when they face setbacks (*https://my.mindprintlearning.com/toolbox/toolbox-demo/product/11786*).

For students with a fixed mindset, achievement might be viewed as beyond their control because "I'm not smart enough" or "I'm just not good at this." They might not put in the required effort because they do not believe they will be successful. With bright students, it might mean doing just enough to look good without risking making a mistake, or not trying if there is a risk they might not succeed. For self-regulated learning to be successful, students must be willing to put in the required effort without consistent prodding, and this drive comes from a true belief that they are in control of their own growth and success. The desire to be better must come from within.

VITAL VOCAB

mindset: A concept researched by Stanford Professor Carol Dweck (*www.ted.com/talks/carol_dweck_the_power_of_believing_that_you_can_improve*) showing that your beliefs about your ability to learn can have a significant impact on achievement.

fixed mindset: Belief that one's capabilities and talents are mostly fixed and will not change significantly with effort.

growth mindset: Belief that capabilities can be developed through effort and an ongoing willingness to try new strategies, accept feedback, and adapt.

TEACHER TAKEAWAYS

- While there are some aspects of growth mindset that can be taught, growth mindset should be viewed as a set of thought processes that must be continuously nurtured and developed.

- Instilling growth mindset requires consistency and ongoing reinforcement for good effort, risk taking, and the ability to persevere until you succeed.

- Growth and improvement require an understanding of *how* you work best, what specific strategies will enable you to succeed, and a willingness to keep trying new approaches until you achieve success.

STUDENT TAKEAWAYS

- Your mindset, or how you view your ability to learn and grow, will have a big impact on your ultimate success, regardless of your starting point.

- If you want to improve, you need to be open to taking feedback and adjusting. The most successful students are those willing to listen and make changes.

- Growth mindset is not only about working hard, but also about working smart. This process will help you discover how to work more efficiently, focus your efforts, and continue to grow and succeed. However, you must be open to feedback and willing to change.

MINDPRINT STRATEGIES FOR STUDENTS

- Remind Students You Believe in Them (*https://my.mindprintlearning.com/toolbox/toolbox-demo/product/12206*) (T)

- Throw Away Test Anxiety (*https://my.mindprintlearning.com/toolbox/toolbox-demo/product/1997*) (T, S)

- Share True Stories (*https://my.mindprintlearning.com/toolbox/toolbox-demo/product/12183*) (T)

- Teach to Speak Up About Needs (*https://my.mindprintlearning.com/toolbox/toolbox-demo/product/11514*) (T, S)

- Encourage and Learn from Mistakes (*https://my.mindprintlearning.com/toolbox/toolbox-demo/product/11786*) (T)

A CLOSER LOOK

- Articles on Growth Mindset; Mindprint Learning (*mindprintlearning.com/article/topics/academic-potential/grit-growth-mindset/*)

- Brainology/Mindset Works Free Resources; Mindset Works (*www.mindsetworks.com/Free-Resources/*)

LESSON ACTIVITIES

Direct Instruction

What is growth mindset? (E, M, H)

Teacher-Led Discussion

Review the Science of Learning lesson as appropriate.

Growth mindset is about continuous improvement and understanding. We all have the power to strengthen our brains by putting forth the effort, taking feedback, and using the right strategies to adjust and improve.

Making mistakes is a necessary part of growth and improvement. No one tries new things and gets them right the first time. If you are not making mistakes, you are not stretching your mind and growing. Everyone in this room, in the world, has plenty of opportunity for growth. So, if you're not making mistakes, you aren't doing your job as a learner, and I'm not doing my job as a teacher.

Teacher Example

Give a personal example about something you learned by working hard and using strategies to overcome challenges. The more personal and the more details, the more likely your story will resonate.

Explain what you wanted to accomplish and why it was important to you.

Highlight how you put forth effort.

Highlight how you had to use a combination or try different strategies to achieve your goal.

Include a mistake you made and how it helped you grow. If it is funny, even better. It is crucial for students to accept mistakes with good humor.

Student Activity

Have students fill out the following Sharing & Storytelling worksheet and then share in pairs in groups of three, or in class discussion. (E, M, H)

Student Activity

You create the class poster I Can Help Myself Grow! with the Fixed Mindset column all or partially filled in. Include subject-specific items as appropriate.

Students fill in the Growth Mindset column and any other ideas for Fixed Mindset. Hang in the classroom and refer to the poster for ongoing coaching. (E, M, H)

Student Activity

Everyone Makes Mistakes: Have students find a quote from someone famous that addresses growth mindset. Ask them to explain how the quote is relevant to something they have done in the past or want to do in the future. Then students can write, draw a picture, or make a video depicting that quote. (E, M, H)

Student Activity

I Can Be Famous: Ask students to choose a biography of someone famous and have them answer and discuss the questions. Reading a true story can help students appreciate that success requires hard work, overcoming obstacles, and resilience in response to failures. (E, M, H)

Student Activity

Have students watch and discuss Ted Talk: Write Your Story, Change History, by Brad Meltzer (*www.youtube.com/watch?v=9LR7Vb6mqts*). Focus on the message, "Dream big, work hard, stay humble." (M, H)

STUDENT ACTIVITY: Sharing & Storytelling

Name: _____

In one or two sentences, describe a problem or something new you tried.

_____
_____
_____
_____

List 3-4 things you did to solve the problem or overcome a challenge. How did you work hard, practice, or use strategies to succeed?

1. _____
2. _____
3. _____
4. _____

Mistakes happen. List 1-2 mistakes or things that went wrong along the way and what you did to correct them.

1. _____
2. _____

What did you learn from the experience? How have you changed or improved as a result?

_____
_____
_____
_____

STUDENT ACTIVITY:
I Can Help Myself Grow!

Name: _____

FIXED MINDSET	GROWTH MINDSET
Instead of…	**I can say…**
I can't do it	
This is too hard	
I'm bad at…	
It didn't work. I give up!	
That's so easy for me	
This is good enough	
Add your own:	

STUDENT ACTIVITY:
Everyone Makes Mistakes

Name: _____

Select a quote from someone famous that reflects growth mindset. You will find some options below or you can find your own. How is that quote relevant to an experience you have had or a goal you hope to achieve? Draw a picture, create a video, or write about why the quote is meaningful to you.

"Nothing great was ever achieved without enthusiasm."

—RALPH WALDO EMERSON

"You miss 100% of the shots you don't take."

—WAYNE GRETZKY

"I've missed more than 9,000 shots in my career. I've lost almost 300 games. Twenty-six times, I've been trusted to take the game-winning shot and missed. I've failed over and over and over again in my life. And that is why I succeed."

—MICHAEL JORDAN

"I have not failed. I have just found 10,000 ways that won't work."

—THOMAS EDISON

"Insanity: Doing the same thing over and over again, and expecting different results."

—ALBERT EINSTEIN

"Success is only meaningful and enjoyable if it feels like your own."

—MICHELLE OBAMA

"Success is not final, failure is not fatal: it is the courage to continue that counts."

—WINSTON CHURCHILL

"There are no secrets to success. It is the result of preparation, hard work, and learning from failure."

—COLIN POWELL

STUDENT ACTIVITY:
I Can Be Famous

Name: _____

Choose a biography of someone you would like to learn more about. After you finish reading, answer the following questions.

What was the person's original life goal? Did they meet their goal? Surpass it? Achieve a different goal?
_____
_____

What major obstacles did the person need to overcome to become successful?
_____
_____

What key personal characteristics enabled him/her to achieve the goal?
_____
_____

Who was important in helping him/her achieve the goal?
_____
_____

Why do you think he or she was successful whereas others were not as successful?
_____
_____
_____

What traits do you share with this person?
_____
_____

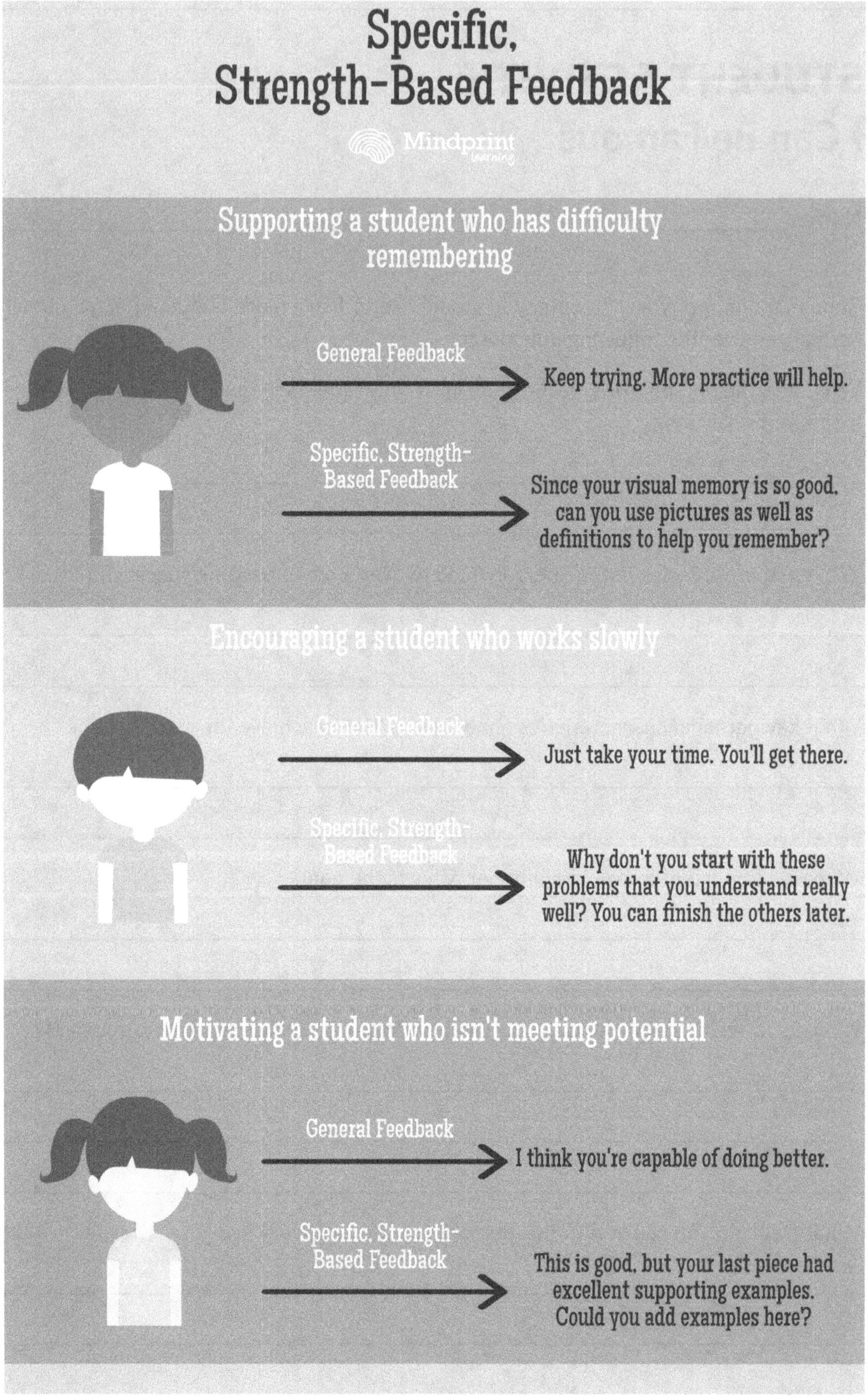

Figure 5: Strength-based feedback

Lesson 3

Nurturing a Growth Mindset

Students need ongoing reinforcement to sustain a growth mindset. Growing up is hard! They need encouragement to continue to take risks and not fear mistakes. Much of this reinforcement happens in the way you talk to and support your students.

VITAL VOCAB

grit: Another term for resilience and perseverance, coined in this context by Angela Duckworth (Duckworth, 2006).

resilience: The ability to recover from difficulties or setbacks and respond with a positive attitude.

risk taking: The willingness to take on challenges despite uncertainty of the result or reward.

TEACHER TAKEAWAYS

- ☐ It is important to give students opportunities to take risks without fear of being laughed at or getting a bad grade. They need to experience the rewards of risk taking.

- ☐ Word choice is important, but so is sincerity. You should praise effort and outcomes tied to strong effort, but only if the effort is truly praiseworthy. Do not praise all effort and all outcomes; otherwise, the praise will no longer be meaningful.

STUDENT TAKEAWAYS

- Growth mindset is not just about effort—you grow your brain and work toward your goals by trying, practicing, taking risks, and learning from your mistakes.

- If you catch yourself thinking, "I can't," replace it with, "What strategy should I try so I can?"

- Everyone makes mistakes and experiences setbacks. It is how you respond to disappointments that determines how much you grow, improve, and ultimately, succeed.

 MINDPRINT STRATEGIES FOR STUDENTS

- Avoid Stereotype Threat (*https://my.mindprintlearning.com/toolbox/toolbox-demo/product/12119*) (T)

- Balanced, Specific Feedback (*https://my.mindprintlearning.com/toolbox/toolbox-demo/product/11503*) (T)

- Give Feedback Based on Personality & Mastery Level (*https://my.mindprintlearning.com/toolbox/toolbox-demo/product/12321*) (T)

- Positive Self-Talk (*https://my.mindprintlearning.com/toolbox/toolbox-demo/product/11889*) (S)

- Coach How to Take Feedback (*https://my.mindprintlearning.com/toolbox/toolbox-demo/product/12262*) (T)

A CLOSER LOOK

- Brainology/Mindset Works Free Resources; Mindset Works (*www.mindsetworks.com/Free-Resources/*)

- Why Project-Based Learning? Buck Institute for Education (*www.bie.org*)

- Grit Scale; Dr. Angela Duckworth (*angeladuckworth.com/grit-scale/*)

LESSON ACTIVITIES

Student Activity

Have students watch and discuss this Ted Talk by Harry Potter author J. K. Rowling (*www.ted.com/talks/jk_rowling_the_fringe_benefits_of_failure*), who explains her many failures before her unparalleled success. (M, H)

Student Activity

Have students participate in Project-Based Learning (*my.mindprintlearning.com/toolbox/toolbox-demo/product/12101*), an approach that supports risk taking, learning through trial and error, and growth mindset. (E, M, H)

Coaching

Classroom Culture: Create a classroom environment that incorporates student choice, leadership, inquiry, initiation, and independent thinking. Students will grow more comfortable taking risks. Encourage student inquiry via open-ended questions (*https://my.mindprintlearning.com/toolbox/toolbox-demo/product/10179*) and modeling curiosity with What If (*https://my.mindprintlearning.com/toolbox/toolbox-demo/product/12233*). (E, M, H)

Coaching

Celebrate Risk: When a student takes a risk, point it out either privately or publicly and celebrate it, even if the student might not have been entirely successful. You might offer elementary-age students a sticker each time. (E, M, H)

Coaching

Grade-Free Assignments: Give assignments that will not be graded. After successful completion, have students reflect on what they did, why they did it, and what motivated them to put forth the effort. (E, M, H)

Coaching

Speaking Growth Mindset: Offering regular specific feedback and encouragement is essential to fostering a growth mindset. Feedback should be honest, balanced, and constructive. Just as students need to possess self-awareness of their individual strengths and how to work effectively, the feedback that we give them as educators also needs to be specific so that students understand not only what needs to improve but also how to improve. (E, M, H)

Points to Keep in Mind when Providing Feedback

Praise the effort, not the outcome. Be specific about why it was a good effort, and identify strategies students used effectively. Don't say, "Great job! You worked really hard." Instead, say, "You spaced out your studying and didn't cram for the test this time. That was a great approach. If you keep it up, your grades will continue to improve."

Help students find and use strategies based on their strengths (*https://my.mindprintlearning.com/toolbox/toolbox-demo/product/11582*). "You are studying really hard for this vocabulary test. Since you remember things so well with pictures, try finding a picture for each word that will help you remember and put it on a flashcard."

Model positive thinking (*https://my.mindprintlearning.com/toolbox/toolbox-demo/product/11889*) and verbalize your own use of strategies out loud. "I did not get out the door on time this morning, but tomorrow I'm going to plan out my morning using a checklist and that will help me get organized."

Help your students view setbacks or mistakes as a steppingstone (*https://my.mindprintlearning.com/toolbox/toolbox-demo/product/11786*) to future success. Every successful person has stories of the failures he or she had to overcome along the way. Acknowledge the obstacles while offering specific tools and strategies to help overcome them. Reinforce that when students are not successful, how they respond can be just as important as the outcome.

Provide relevant examples of your own mistakes and failures. Stories can be the most powerful way to reach students.

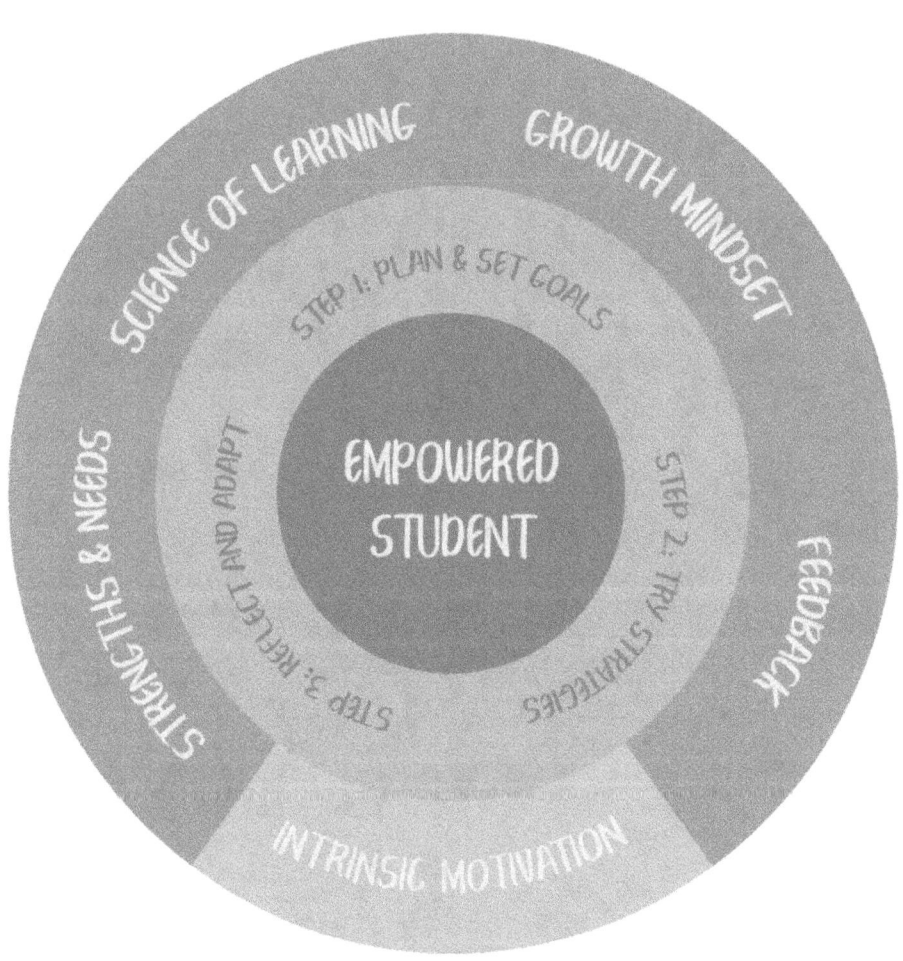

Figure 6: Intrinsic motivation

Lesson 4

Intrinsic Motivation

Motivation plays a key role in the process of successful learning. External factors like achieving good grades and pleasing others can work as short-term motivators and can even help to push students toward long-term success. However, extrinsic motivators like grades or special treats can start to lose value after elementary school for many students (Kohn, 1993). They can also lead to excessive stress or anxiety.

In contrast, intrinsic motivators develop from our own unique passions, interests, and reasons for wanting to learn and work hard. Successful outcomes driven by intrinsic motivation lead to self-confidence and the enthusiasm to persevere, even in the face of setbacks.

VITAL VOCAB

extrinsic motivation: Behavior that is driven by external rewards such as grades and praise. This type of motivation arises from outside the individual, often from a parent, a teacher, or a material reward.

intrinsic motivation: Behavior that is driven by internal rewards, such as feelings of fulfillment, pleasure, and interest.

TEACHER TAKEAWAYS

- ☐ Extrinsic motivators like grades, a gold star, or special treats can help younger students be compliant and learn. However, those rewards are far less effective in higher grades.

- ☐ The best way to develop intrinsic motivation is to help students identify their personal interests, strengths, and goals. Help them see how working on a given assignment or subject can be tied to achieving their long-term goals.

- ☐ When possible, give students a choice in projects and assignments. Choice instills ownership and increases the likelihood they will be interested, motivated, and successful.

 ## STUDENT TAKEAWAYS

- ☐ Ultimately your life satisfaction depends on discovering what motivates you, not on satisfying your teachers, parents, or friends.

- ☐ When you enjoy what you do, you are far more likely to be successful. Take time to discover what you enjoy. Try not to worry about what others are doing or thinking.

 MINDPRINT STRATEGIES FOR STUDENTS

- Develop Intrinsic Motivation (*https://my.mindprintlearning.com/toolbox/toolbox-demo/product/11337*) (T)

- Project-Based Learning (PBL) (*https://my.mindprintlearning.com/toolbox/toolbox-demo/product/12101*) (T)

- Tools for Project-Based Learning (*https://my.mindprintlearning.com/toolbox/uid/search?name=&academic_topics=504&cognitive_skills=&interests=&product_types=2.4.5.6.7.8.9&age_range_min=3&age_range_max=21&order_by=bestfit_score+desc&uses_recommendations=&pills=academic_topics%7C504*) (T)

A CLOSER LOOK

- Articles on Intrinsic Motivation; Mind/Shift (*ww2.kqed.org/mindshift/tag/intrinsic-motivation/*)

- 6 Tips for Getting Started with Genius Hour; Edutopia (*www.edutopia.org/groups/personalized-learning/802456*)

- Ideas for Genius Hour; Genius Hour (*www.geniushour.com*)

- Articles on Grit, Growth Mindset, and Intrinsic Motivation; Mindprint Learning (*mindprintlearning.com/article/topics/academic-potential/grit-growth-mindset/*)

LESSON ACTIVITIES

Direct Instruction

Motivation: Discuss the difference between intrinsic and extrinsic motivation. (E, M, H)

Student Activity

Watch and discuss Logan LaPlant's TEDx Talk: Hackschooling Makes Me Happy (*www.youtube.com/watch?v=h11u3vtcpaY*). Discuss the role students can play in taking control of their own learning. (E, M)

Student Activity

My Interests and Passions: Students complete exercise and teachers can use responses to support lesson planning. (E, M, H)

Student Activity

Classroom Rules/Commandments: Consider as a start-of-the-term activity. Have the class brainstorm ideas for class rules either independently or as a group. As a class, narrow down or prioritize the rules that will be most important for successful, self-regulated learning. Post the final rules in the classroom. Giving students some control over the classroom environment is a first step in allowing them to take control of their overall learning. (E, M)

Student Activity

Choose an App: Allow students to search their Mindprint Toolbox by interest and choose an app or website to play during class or for homework. Afterward, you can ask students why they chose the app they did and what they learned. (E, M)

Coaching

Choice Assignments: Offer assignments that allow students to choose their topic and/or their presentation format. Project-based learning is a great approach to support student interest and choice. Incorporate Genius Hour (*www.geniushour.com*) into your class curriculum, setting aside an hour a week for students to work on an independent passion project. (E, M, H)

Teacher-led Discussion

Explain how incorporating things you enjoy into your learning, or learning to find them within activities, helps make school more interesting and motivating. When thinking about what you enjoy, students should think about not only hobbies or activities they are already involved in, but also topics, causes, and ideas they like thinking about.

Give examples of how their interests can lead to something else. For example: an interest in hands-on construction can lead to using blocks/cubes to help with solving math problems; an interest in drawing can lead to illustrating when taking notes; or an interest in animals can be taken into consideration when choosing books to read or a research topic.

Discuss the importance of "feeling" your interests rather than focusing on grades or what friends are doing.

Brainstorm a list of extrinsic vs. intrinsic motivators and discuss them in class.

Be prepared that this conversation could easily evolve into a discussion of the importance of grades versus learning and the stress that students might be feeling.

Teacher Example

Give an example of a passion of your own and relate it to choices you have made in your own learning.

Consider explaining how your passions or interests led you to teaching a specific subject, working with children, or pursuing a hobby.

Talk about how you discovered your passion—was it something you always just knew, or how did you go about discovering it?

STUDENT ACTIVITY:
My Interests and Passions

Name: _____

Use the space below to write a list of the activities, topics, and thoughts that interest you or that you would like to learn more about. If you have time, write about how you would like to apply those interests in this class.

STUDENT ACTIVITY:
Classroom Rules/Commandments

Name: _____

Take a few minutes to brainstorm class rules for the semester. With your classmates, discuss and prioritize those rules. How will you self-monitor and help each other stick to them throughout the semester?

Figure 7: Metacognition, the key to a growth mindset

Lesson 5

Developing Self-Awareness

Students cannot effectively take responsibility and ownership of their learning unless they have good self-awareness. Self-awareness in learning is known as metacognition. Developing metacognition takes time. Teachers and parents can help by continuously reinforcing the need for students to think about their thinking: Why did I try that approach? Why did I do well on that test? How did I study? Did it work? Without metacognition, students might have a positive mindset and work hard, but they will not know how to work most effectively and efficiently. Developing self-awareness skills is an essential step in developing purposeful, motivated learners.

VITAL VOCAB

metacognition: Understanding of one's own thinking. Metacognition includes an awareness of learning processes and strategies you use as well as an understanding of your personal strengths and needs.

self-awareness: The ability to recognize and assess one's own feelings, thought processes, and behaviors.

self-monitoring: Measuring, evaluating, and adjusting one's own behavior, thoughts, and feelings in relation to expected age-appropriate norms.

TEACHER TAKEAWAYS

- Students need to grow into the habit of thinking about their thinking and learning. It is important for students to develop self-awareness of what they do and do not understand and why. Students must learn to recognize when they need to seek help and what type of help they need.

- Most students need to learn how to self-assess. Stronger students tend to underestimate their mastery and overstudy, which can lead to excessive stress or anxiety. Struggling students tend to overestimate their mastery and might not study enough or study the wrong things, which can lead to underperformance (Kruger & Dunning, 1999).

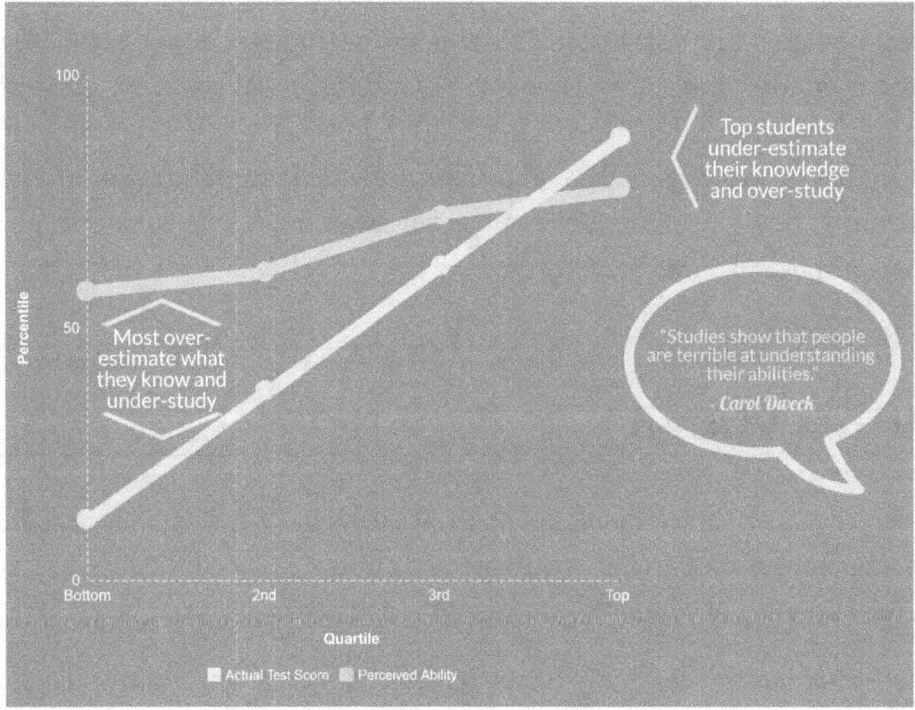

Figure 8: The Dunning-Kruger Effect

- Metacognitive thinking is important not only in academic learning but for all of life's experiences.

- Metacognition leads to empathy—the better you understand yourself, the more you can relate to others and understand their perspectives.

- Metacognitive thinking develops over time. Adult nurturing and support through ongoing, objective feedback helps significantly.

STUDENT TAKEAWAYS

- When you focus not just on the outcome but also on why you did well or not, you are more likely to improve in subsequent attempts.

- When you understand and accept your own strengths and challenges, it will be easier to relate to your classmates during group work and social situations.

- Although you know yourself better than anyone, you are still learning and growing. Sometimes adults and friends will see you in a way that you do not see yourself. It is important for you to listen to feedback to fully and effectively self-assess.

- Most students struggle to find the right balance of what to study and how much. You don't want to study too little, but you also don't want to overstudy. It is important to learn to recognize when you need to work harder or longer and when you can feel confident in your knowledge and mastery.

 MINDPRINT STRATEGIES FOR STUDENTS

- Self-Awareness (Metacognition) (*https://my.mindprintlearning.com/toolbox/toolbox-demo/product/10345*) (S)

- Instill Ownership in Class Work (*https://my.mindprintlearning.com/toolbox/toolbox-demo/product/11909*) (T)

- Dialogue Journal (*https://my.mindprintlearning.com/toolbox/toolbox-demo/product/10421*) (T, S)

- Exam Wrapper (*https://my.mindprintlearning.com/toolbox/toolbox-demo/product/11537*) (T)

A CLOSER LOOK

- Mindprint Homework Wrappers by Skill (*https://s3.amazonaws.com/wordpress_uploads/site/uploads/2014/04/mindprint-homework-wrappers.pdf*)

- 5 Strategies on Teaching Students to Use Metacognition; teachthought (*www.teachthought.com/learning/5-strategies-teaching-students-use-metacognition/*)

- Nurturing Self-Awareness in the Classroom; edutopia (*www.edutopia.org/blog/8-pathways-metacognition-in-classroom-marilyn-price-mitchell*)

- Exit Slips, Robert Marzano of ASCD (*www.ascd.org/publications/educational-leadership/oct12/vol70/num02/The-Many-Uses-of-Exit-Slips.aspx*)

LESSON ACTIVITIES

Direct Instruction

What Is Metacognition? (E, M, H)

Teacher Background:

Metacognition is one of the most important skills in the process of building self-regulated learning and driving student success. You can make it important by making it practical. Start by simply defining it for them. Then practice and develop it in the context of everyday learning. Well-developed metacognition evolves over time. Expect that a deeper understanding and appreciation will come with practice.

Teacher-led Discussion:

Start with the definition. Describe it simply as: *"Metacognition is thinking about your thinking"* or more detailed, *"...thinking about your thinking to improve your learning."*

Highlight that although students might understand a concept, they come to that understanding in their own unique way.

Understanding your own processes will help make it easier for you to learn new things.

Teacher Example:

Give a personal example of how you understood a problem or situation differently from someone else, even though you both had the same information. The funnier the outcome, the better!

Work through a problem on the board and discuss how you are thinking about it: *If you make a mistake, how do you think about correcting it?* On an ongoing basis, remember to think aloud. Regularly ask the class if anyone was thinking about the problem differently or has an alternate way to solve the problem.

You can model metacognition by asking yourself the questions in Figure 9 aloud when providing feedback and instruction. Over time, students will begin asking themselves these questions.

Student Activity

Self-control and self-awareness are closely aligned. Watch and discuss Ted Talk: Don't Eat the Marshmallow (www.ted.com/talks/joachim_de_posada_says_don_t_eat_the_marshmallow_yet) as the start of a discussion on self-awareness. (M, H)

Student Activity

This Is What I'm Thinking: Have students fill out this sheet independently. Use a relatively brief exercise so students have the mental energy to focus on the metacognitive task and not be tired from learning. Plan to do this activity several times so that students grow more accustomed to thinking about their thinking and ways to improve. Discussing students' responses with them individually is optimal. For ongoing coaching, prompts can be posted on a class poster and copies can be printed for students to complete during assignments. (E, M, H)

Student Activity

Dialogue Journal: Use between student and teacher as a written discussion throughout the term. Give each student his or her own journal. The frequency of writing and responding depends on the class subject and how often it meets. If a class meets every day, it might make sense for the student to write in the journal

1–2 times per week. Teachers give a specific prompt and guidelines about what is expected (e.g., a one-sentence answer or a one-page reflection). To inspire metacognitive thinking and reflection, consider the best prompts to encourage students to think about their academic experiences and learning in a way that is most relevant and comfortable. Teachers should expect to respond to each student promptly and model the types of responses they expect in their answers. Teacher responses could include questions for the student to reflect further. (E, M, H)

Student Activity

Show Your Thinking: Have students use one of the many apps available that allow them to show and record their thinking—e.g., ThinkingKit (*https://my.mindprintlearning.com/toolbox/toolbox-demo/product/12284*) or Storyboard That (*https://my.mindprintlearning.com/toolbox/toolbox-demo/product/11295*). (E, M, H)

Student Activity

Exit Slip: Use this activity as a short reflection at the end of class so that students have an immediate opportunity to reflect on what they learned. Provide a page with no more than three prompts that are relevant to the class or lesson. Depending on your goals and time, you can ask for simple fill-in-the-blank answers (e.g., The hardest thing I did today was _____) or require students to go further and explain why. This daily reflection can be modified to be a weekly reflection. You can do it as a group dice game, where each prompt corresponds to a number on the die. Students take a turn rolling and sharing based on the roll. Alternatively, exam wrappers (*https://my.mindprintlearning.com/toolbox/toolbox-demo/product/11537*) can be used after quizzes or tests. (E, M, H)

Coaching

Metacognitive Questions: Referring to the prompts on the image, model metacognitive thought processes out loud as you teach. Talk through your thinking and problem solving steps: "Hmmm. Where did I make my mistake? I tried this but it didn't work…" Point out when a student is using metacognition. Repeat what the student said and label it as "using metacognition." You might even have a "metacognitive thinking" board and post examples when they arise in class. This might come up if a student is reflecting on why they had difficulty on an assignment or a test. (E, M, H)

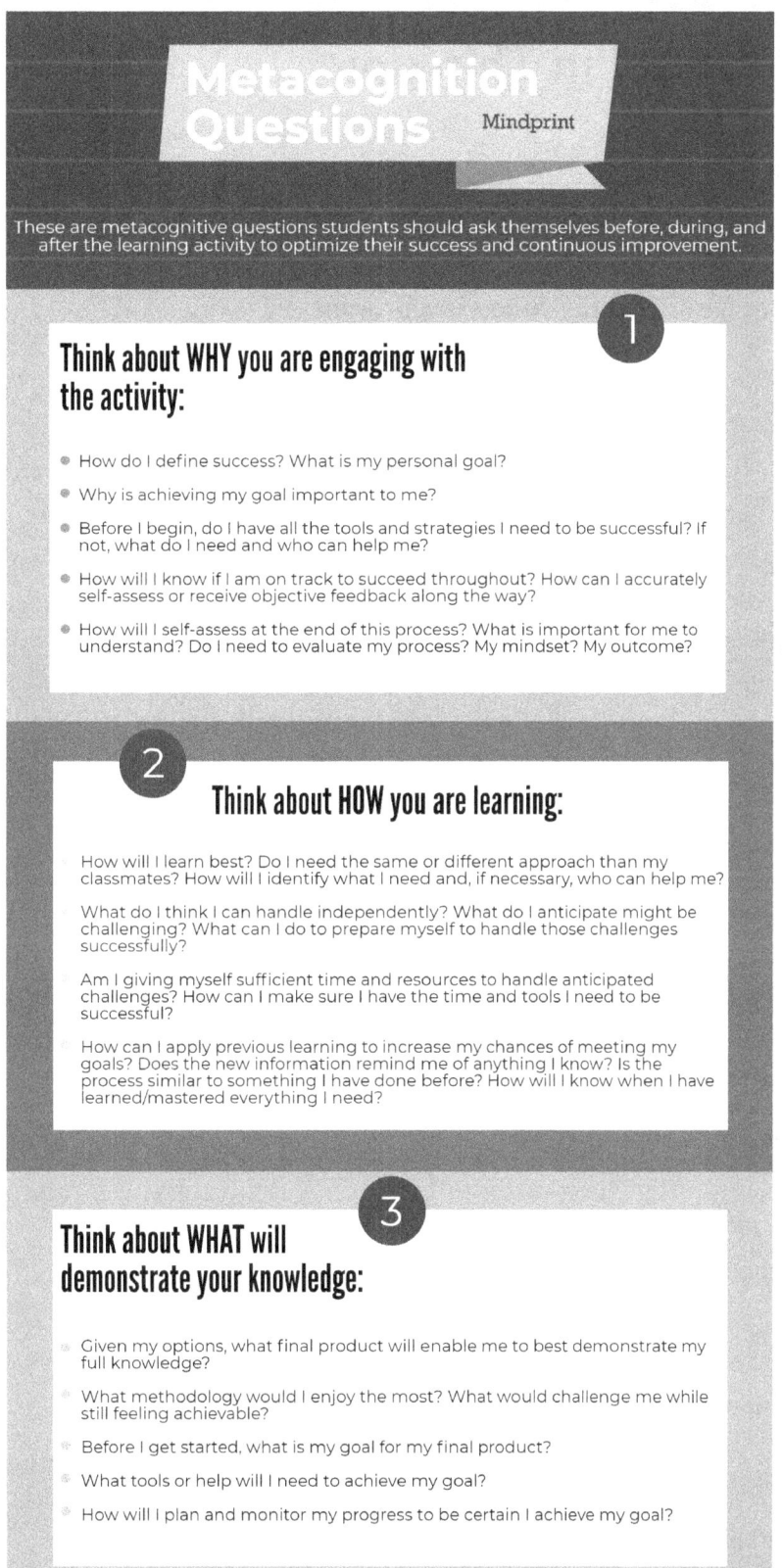

Figure 9: Metacognition questions

STUDENT ACTIVITY:
This Is What I'm Thinking

Name: _____

Respond to at least 2 of the following prompts:

I'm wondering…

I'm picturing…

I am reminded of…

I understood it best when…

I liked when…

Respond to at least 2 of the following prompts:

I have questions about…

I want to go back to…

I am confused about…

I had difficulty when…

STUDENT ACTIVITY:
Dialogue Journal

Provide students with one or two of the following prompts each time you ask them to write in their journals. Students might enjoy selecting or personalizing their journal covers at the beginning of the term.

Today I learned…

Today I was most interested in…Why?

One thing I did differently today was…How did it turn out?

One risk I took today was…How did it turn out?

Something that was hard for me was…Why? How did I take on the challenge?

I didn't understand…What did I do?

I have more questions about…How will I answer those?

I used a new strategy today…What was it? How did it go?

Next time I will try…

STUDENT ACTIVITY:
Exit Slip

Name: _____

Think about your work in class today and respond to at least two of the following:

Today I learned…

I want to investigate further…

I am still wondering…

I am proud of…

Next time I will do this differently…

I keep thinking about…

I was surprised by…

I did not understand…

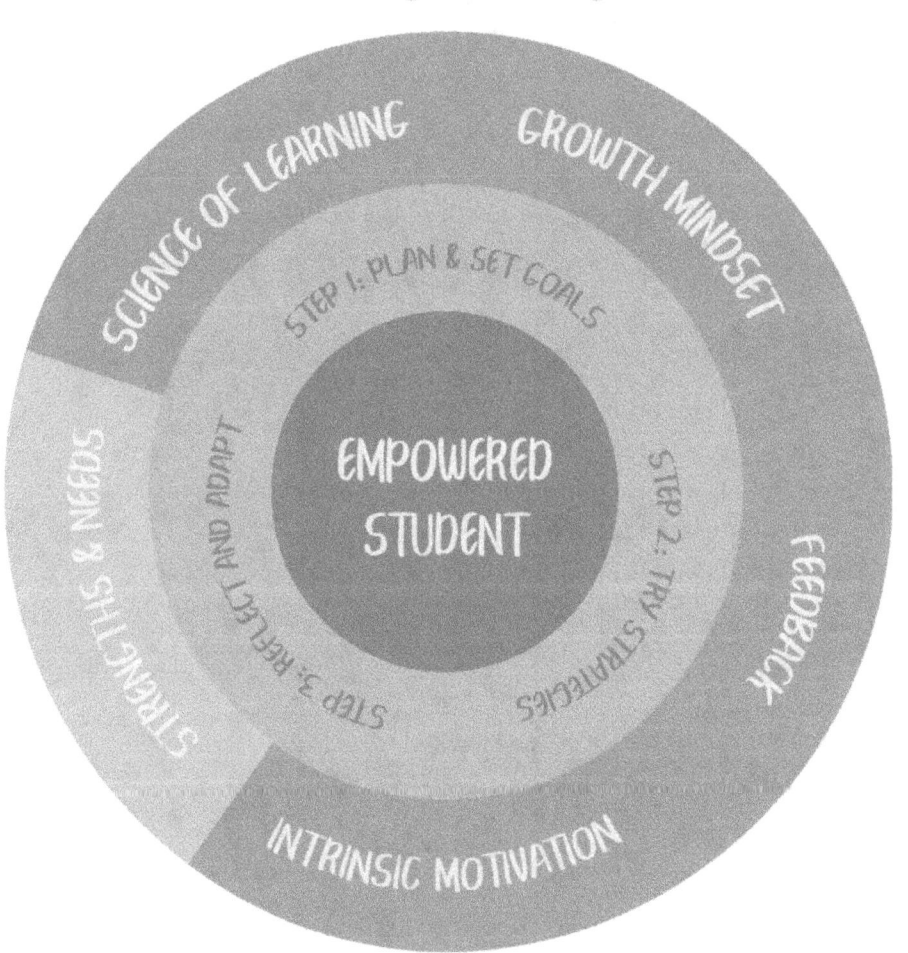

Figure 10: Understanding strengths and needs

Lesson 6

Understanding Strengths and Needs

The most successful learners have a realistic understanding of their strengths and needs across three broad interdependent sets of skills: academic skills, personal skills, and cognitive skills. Historically, educators might have focused only on teaching academic skills, such as reading, writing, math, history, and science. Although academic skill mastery was arguably the ultimate objective of a K–12 education, little attention was paid to why students weren't mastering academic skills. Rather than looking at variability of learner needs, educators usually provided more repetition in the same format.

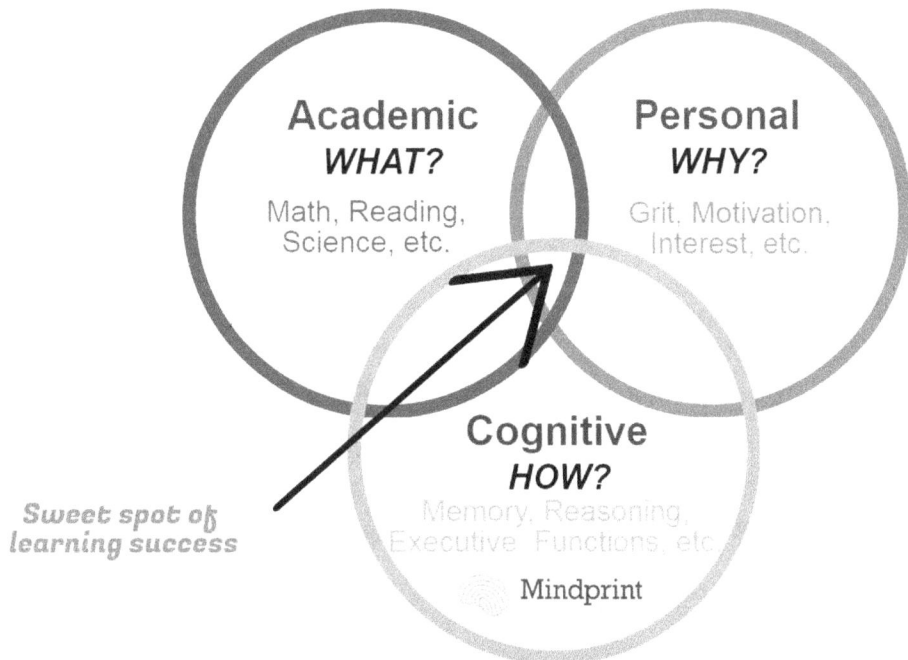

Figure 11: Sweet spot of learning success

Fortunately, through the efforts of educational researchers, there is a much greater focus on understanding a student's personal interests and needs to improve learning outcomes (Harackiewicz & Hulleman, 2010). When students have an inherent interest in what they are learning, they are more likely to understand and remember.

Unfortunately, it's impractical to always appeal to a student's intrinsic interests. Students are expected (for good reason) to achieve mastery of foundational knowledge across subjects, not just the subjects they enjoy the most. When students must learn in areas in which they have little inherent interest, researchers such as Dr. Angela Duckworth and Dr. Carol Dweck have taught us the importance of personal skills that can ultimately differentiate the most successful students from their equally able peers. Duckworth refers to this personality trait as "grit," Dweck focuses on "mindset," and other researchers focus on such variations as perseverance, resilience, and social-emotional skills.

Their research teaches us that when students are willing to work hard, take responsibility for learning in a variety of settings, and respond positively to obstacles, they are far more likely to achieve academic success. The research is also clear that these personal skills are subject to considerable environmental influence (Center on the Developing Child, Harvard University, 2017). Although some students might be naturally "grittier" than others, adults can play a critical role in nurturing and fostering the personal skills that every student needs to succeed. However, it is also clear that students enter classrooms with variability that extends far beyond personal and academic skills.

Cognitive skills might be the most researched and yet least discussed in educational environments. They are the "invisible skills" that students use to access, understand, interpret, and apply information across subjects. They include long-term memory, complex reasoning, executive functions, and processing speed, and they provide the clearest insight into variability among learners.

Insight into a student's cognitive strengths and needs enables educators to anticipate which academic skills a student will learn with ease or difficulty, and how to adapt instruction accordingly. The more teachers know about a student's cognitive skills, the more effective they can be with giving each student the best options for perceiving, comprehending and mastering new information. What's more, researchers know that cognitive skills are far less influenced by age and environment than are academic and personal skills (Passler, Beinecke, & Hell, 2015). When we help students to understand their cognitive strengths and needs, we provide them with a stable foundation on which to grow their self-awareness of what they need to become successful learners. They learn how they can make the best choices to learn in any situation.

💬 VITAL VOCAB

academic skills: Learned knowledge such as how to structure an essay, important dates in history, and algebra. Referred to in the research as crystallized or learned ability or general knowledge.

cognitive skills: Skills that explain how you learn most efficiently, including memory, reasoning, and attention. These skills don't typically change as much as academic and personal skills, but they do mature throughout adolescence and into early adulthood. Referred to in the research as fluid ability.

habits of mind: A subset of personal skills, habits of mind involve one's disposition or feelings toward tasks. This skill set encompasses terms including resilience, mindset, and grit.

personal skills: Skills that explain how you feel and interact with people and the environment. Like cognitive skills, these skills develop and mature throughout adolescence and into adulthood. Sometimes they are called social-emotional or "soft skills" in contrast to the "hard skills" of academic knowledge.

whole child: A body of research showing the importance of understanding students' full set of skills—personal, cognitive, and academic—to help them learn effectively.

TEACHER TAKEAWAYS

- ☐ Academic success will depend on addressing not only students' academic needs but their personal needs and interests as well.

- ☐ All students have a unique combination of cognitive skills that can affect their personality and academic success. When students aren't performing to academic potential, it is important to consider personal and cognitive factors to understand how best to support them.

- Each student will come to your classroom with a unique combination of academic, personal, and cognitive strengths and needs. Just because a student is generally strong in one skill does not imply that he or she does not need support in another. All skills are critical to learning. Try to understand each student's unique starting point in each individual skill so you can help him or her grow within each skill.

 STUDENT TAKEAWAYS

- Everyone has strengths. Even if you struggle with a skill or subject, you can still be successful. You might simply need to step back and find a new strategy. It's important that you discover what your strengths are and learn how to use them effectively.

- Everyone has needs, even straight-A students. No one is strong in every skill. Don't expect to be perfect or for everything to be easy. It is important that you acknowledge the more challenging areas so you can ask for help to grow and improve.

- Once you understand and accept your strengths and needs, you can often use your stronger skills to help you succeed. What is most important is that you have a willingness to work hard and keep a positive mindset.

 MINDPRINT STRATEGIES FOR STUDENTS

- Use Strengths to Support Needs (*https://my.mindprintlearning.com/toolbox/toolbox-demo/product/11582*) (T)

- Understanding Test Anxiety (*https://my.mindprintlearning.com/toolbox/toolbox-demo/product/12179*) (T)

- Encourage Reflection (*https://my.mindprintlearning.com/toolbox/toolbox-demo/product/12580*) (T)

Figure 12: World Economic Forum Top 10 Skills in 2020. Source: "The Future of Jobs," World Economic Forum, 2016. From *http://reports.weforum.org/future-of-jobs-2016/*

A CLOSER LOOK

- The 10 Skills You Need to Thrive in the Fourth Industrial Revolution; World Economic Forum (*https://www.weforum.org/agenda/2016/01/the-10-skills-you-need-to-thrive-in-the-fourth-industrial-revolution/*)

- 10 Ways to Nurture the Top Skills of the Future; International Society for Technology in Education (*www.iste.org/explore/articleDetail?articleid=725&category=In-the-classroom&article=*)

- Self-Regulation Using Cognitive Data Is Key to Personalization; edCircuit (*www.edcircuit.com/self-regulation-using-cognitive-data-is-key-to-personalization/*)

LESSON ACTIVITIES

Direct Instruction

Discuss the Sweet Spot of Learning Success graphic after reviewing the definition and examples of the three types of skills (academic, cognitive, personal). Emphasize the importance of having strengths in all these areas for life success.

Student Activity

Sweet Spot of Learning Success: Provide students the opportunity to reflect on a time they were successful because of their academic, personal, and cognitive skills. (E, M, H)

Student Activity

WEF Career Skills Part I: Discuss the World Economic Forum (WEF) skills in the context of students' career aspirations. You can find the definitions on the WEF website (Gray, 2016). Have each student pick a career they might pursue and identify whether they believe the WEF skills will be important for success in that career and why. This can be done as a written exercise, class discussion, or small-group activity. (M, H)

Student Activity

WEF Career Skills Part II: Group students who chose similar careers. Have students discuss which skills they prioritized and what they might do to improve in the skills they believe are most important. (M, H)

Student Activity

This Is Me: Give students the opportunity to reflect on how they perceive themselves. (E, M)

STUDENT ACTIVITY:
Sweet Spot of Learning Success

Think about a time when you had to learn something that was difficult, such as mastering math facts, finishing a very challenging book, studying for a hard chemistry test, learning a new musical piece, or mastering a new art technique. Consider the personal and cognitive skills you used that helped you succeed. Write or make a video about why you succeeded even though it was difficult.

You can use these examples of personal and cognitive skills to get started:

Confident—Believed in myself—Hard-working—Diligent—Dedicated—Never gave up—Optimistic—Not easily discouraged—Gritty—Tough—Persevering—Competitive—Creative—Good memory—Stayed focused—Intense—Efficient—Paid attention—Listened—Flexible—Learned from others—Asked for help—Kept trying—Used good reasoning—Tried alternate approaches—Planned—Managed my time—Took feedback—Collaborative—Motivated

STUDENT ACTIVITY:
WEF Career Skills Part I

Name: _____

I want to be a _____.

Consider if you think each skill is or is not important to success in your identified career. Either write or be prepared to discuss and explain your answers.

WEF SKILLS	THIS SKILL IS/IS NOT IMPORTANT TO MY CAREER. EXPLAIN.
Complex Problem Solving	
Critical Thinking	
Creativity	
People Management	
Coordinating with Others	

WEF SKILLS	THIS SKILL IS/IS NOT IMPORTANT TO MY CAREER. EXPLAIN.
Emotional Intelligence	
Judgment and Decision Making	
Service Orientation	
Negotiation	
Cognitive Flexibility	

STUDENT ACTIVITY:
WEF Career Skills Part II

Work with students who chose a similar career in Part I. Discuss the similarities and differences in your prioritizations. Either individually or as a group, brainstorm what you could do now to develop the skills you prioritized the highest. Brainstorm for at least three skills.

WEF SKILLS	BRAINSTORM IDEAS TO DEVELOP THESE SKILLS
Complex Problem Solving	
Critical Thinking	
Creativity	
People Management	
Coordinating with Others	

WEF SKILLS	BRAINSTORM IDEAS TO DEVELOP THESE SKILLS
Emotional Intelligence	
Judgment and Decision Making	
Service Orientation	
Negotiation	
Cognitive Flexibility	

STUDENT ACTIVITY:
This Is Me

In the following space, brainstorm a list of adjectives that describes you. Include your most positive traits as well as traits you'd like to improve on (e.g., sometimes frustrated, poor speller). When you are done, create a WordCloud (*https://my.mindprintlearning.com/toolbox/toolbox-demo/product/12382*) with your words. Use one color for your positive traits and a different color for the traits you'd like to improve on. Pick a shape for your WordCloud that best reflects how you view yourself.

Figure 13: This Is Me

Having trouble thinking of words to describe you? Ask yourself these questions:

What makes me happy? What is my favorite subject? What activities do I enjoy? How would my friends, parents, teachers describe me? What could I do better in school? At home? What do I find difficult?

My Positive Traits: (minimum of 10)

Skills I Want to Develop: (minimum of 5)

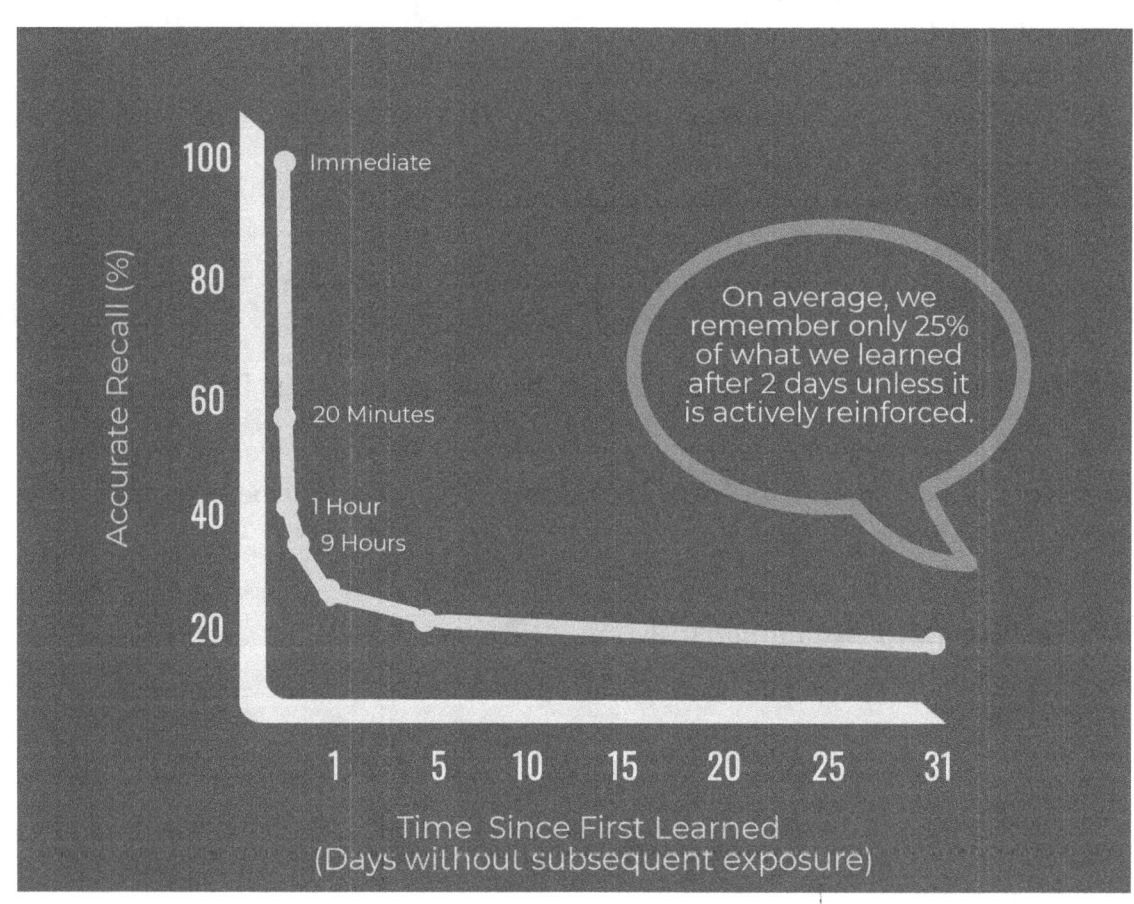

Figure 14: Ebbinghaus's Forgetting Curve. Source: Ebbinghaus, 2013.

Lesson 7

Academic Skills

Academic skills refer to content knowledge learned in school. Some academic skills, such as algebra, are cumulative. Students might learn other academic skills once and then not revisit them unless they are in an area of interest, such as specific events in history. This lesson focuses on helping students develop academic skill mastery for cumulative knowledge building..

VITAL VOCAB

automaticity: Ability to know and recall information without effort, computing, or deliberating. Automaticity is usually the result of repetition and practice.

complex reasoning: Ability to analyze information and solve problems.

fluency: Ability to read or produce an answer to a problem quickly, accurately, automatically, and expressively.

spaced repetition: A learning and memorization technique that incorporates leaving time between repeated review of previously learned material to help your brain practice, absorb, and recall information.

TEACHER TAKEAWAYS

- Certain foundational skills are important for students to have before they can master a subject and use them for higher-level thinking. Other skills and knowledge will be important to know, but it's not essential that students have automaticity with them. Examples of foundational skills include math facts and sight words. Examples of skills not requiring automaticity are details in a novel or subject-specific vocabulary in non-core topics.

- If you find that students are struggling to learn a new skill, it is important to go back and consider if they have automaticity in the prerequisite skills or if the difficulty is in their complex reasoning (a cognitive skill).

- For students who do not seem to be living up to potential or who do better in one subject over another, this can be a good opportunity to understand why these differentials exist. Are key foundational skills missing that are interfering with the student's performance or growth, or is there a different type of underlying challenge (e.g., cognitive or personal)?

 ## STUDENT TAKEAWAYS

- Much of what you will learn in school is cumulative. Therefore, it is important that if you do not understand something you take the time to learn it, even if the test has passed. In many cases, you will need to build on that knowledge for future classes.

- Spaced repetition and practice are essential to learning and remembering foundational skills. Even if you learned something easily, it is important that you continue to practice and reinforce it so you can recall that information when you need it. Remember what you learned about neuroplasticity in Lesson 1.

MINDPRINT STRATEGIES FOR STUDENTS

- Interleave Worked Problems (*https://my.mindprintlearning.com/toolbox/toolbox-demo/product/11910*) (T)

- Spaced Repetition (*https://my.mindprintlearning.com/toolbox/toolbox-demo/product/11427*) (S, T)

- Math Study Skills and Instructional Strategies (*https://my.mindprintlearning.com/toolbox/uid/search?name=math&academic_topics=&cognitive_skills=&interests=&product_types=11.13&age_range_min=3&age_range_max=21&order_by=bestfit_score+desc&uses_recommendations=&pills=&page=1*) (S, T)

- Reading Study Skills and Instructional Strategies (*https://my.mindprintlearning.com/toolbox/uid/search?name=reading&academic_topics=&cognitive_skills=&interests=&product_types=11.13&age_range_min=3&age_range_max=21&order_by=bestfit_score+desc&uses_recommendations=&pills=*) (S, T)

A CLOSER LOOK

- Articles on Math & STEAM (*https://mindprintlearning.com/article/topics/academic-skills/math-stem*)

- Articles on Speaking, Writing, & Spelling (*https://mindprintlearning.com/article/topics/academic-skills/language-speaking-writing*)

- Articles on Reading (*https://mindprintlearning.com/article/topics/academic-skills/reading-vocabulary*)

- Let's Not Forget the Forgetting Curve; Mindprint Learning (*https://mindprintlearning.com/blog/the-forgetting-curve/*)

LESSON ACTIVITIES

Direct Instruction

Overview of Academic Skills and Learning (M, H)

Teacher Background

Communicate the importance of building automaticity of foundational skills, using spaced repetition to ensure retention. Improved automaticity provides students with more mental energy for complex reasoning tasks.

Teacher-led Discussion

Begin with a quick explanation of academic skills so that students can understand how these skills differ from cognitive skills.

Academic skills are what you learn in school.

Much of what you learn in school is cumulative. Be aware of what you did not understand and make sure you take the time to learn it or ask for help, even if the test has passed. Otherwise, it will be harder when that information is pertinent in other contexts.

Show and explain the Forgetting Curve. Remind students that even if they understand and learn new material easily, it does not guarantee they will remember it when they need it.

The Forgetting Curve shows that most people begin to forget in just 20 minutes. So if you feel confident that you remember the material 15 minutes after you studied, see what you can recall after 2 hours or the next day.

Consistent practice and repetition is essential to learning and remembering information. We do this most effectively through spaced repetition, or repeated study/review of material, leaving time in between studying—the opposite of cramming!

Student Activity

Academic Skills Beyond Grades: Help students think about what they truly enjoy learning rather than depending on their grades to tell them. (M, H)

Student Activity

Ask your students questions from past tests. Let them compare their answers on the original test to the most recent one to appreciate how we all forget. This will reinforce the importance of ongoing repetition. (M, H)

Student Activity

Create a Study Schedule for a test the following week. After the test, discuss whether spaced repetition was effective. (M, H)

Student Activity

Use a New Strategy: Have students select up to three strategies from their Personalized Toolbox for either Math or English and add those strategies to their Personal Learning Plans. After a week of using the new strategy in assignments and homework, discuss whether this new strategy is working. Continue this throughout the course. (M, H)

Coaching

Interleaving: Always include questions from previous tests or assignments mixed in within the new material. (E, M, H)

STUDENT ACTIVITY:
Academic Skills Beyond Grades

Name: _____

Grades rarely tell the entire picture of what you know or what you are capable of. Answer at least one of the following questions without referencing past grades.

    Is there a subject or topic that is tough for me? Do I want to improve? Why?

    Is there an area or subject I'm very interested in? What do I want to learn?

    Is there a topic I understand and yet don't do as well as I expect in class or assignments? Why do I think that is?

STUDENT ACTIVITY:
Study Schedule

Name: _____

Write your study plan for how you will prepare for the test.

DAY	WHAT I WILL COVER	TIME NEEDED	COMPLETE
Monday			
Tuesday			
Wednesday			
Thursday			
Friday			
Saturday			
Sunday			

Notes/Reflections:

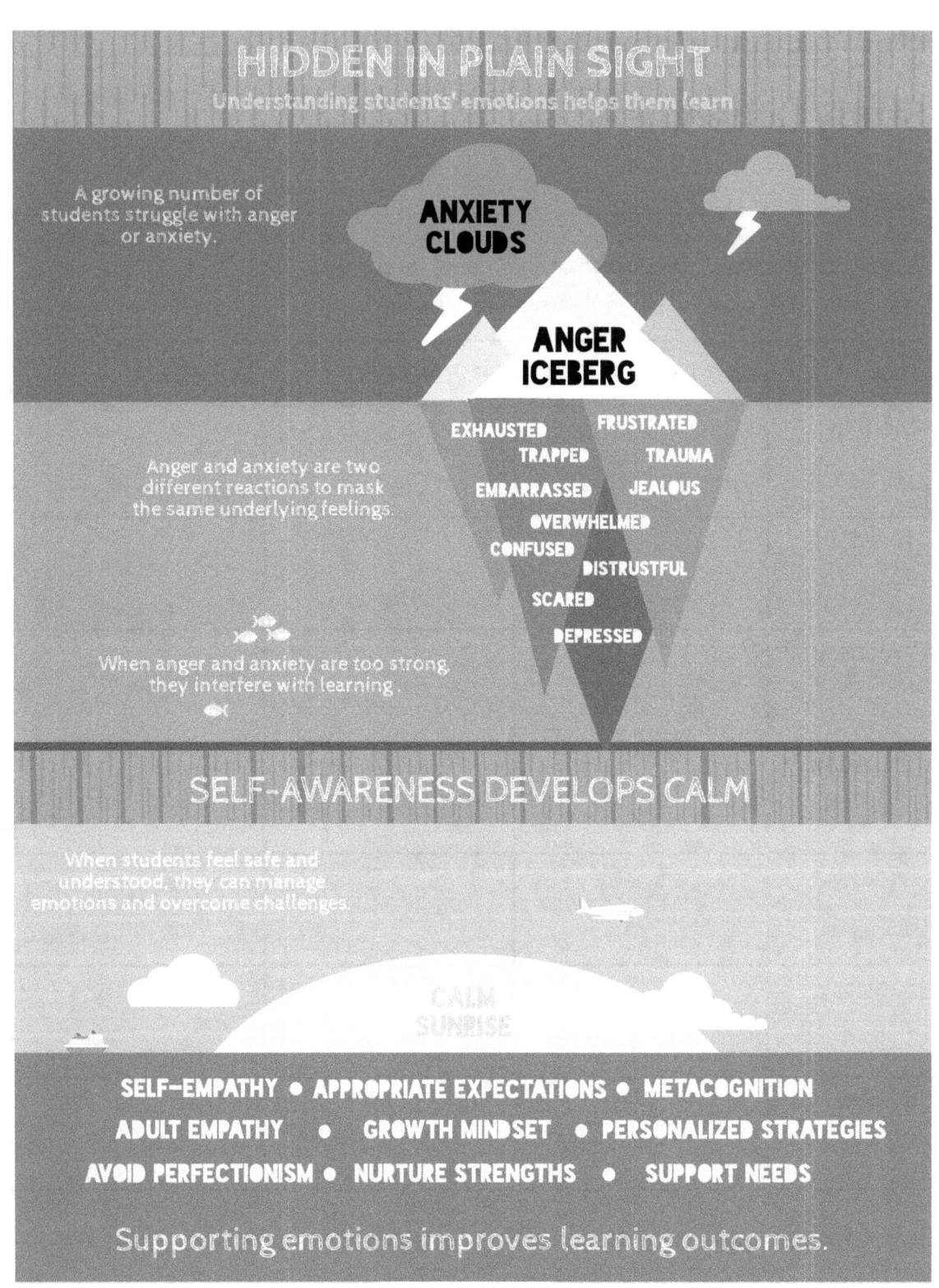

Figure 15: Hidden emotions

Lesson 8

Nonacademic Skills: Personal

If students do not come to class emotionally ready to learn, chances are efficient learning will not happen. We have already covered mindset. The other three factors that tend to have the biggest negative impact on students' academic performance are anger, anxiety, and difficulty collaborating (Lawson, 2002). Help them understand and address these needs.

VITAL VOCAB

adrenaline: A hormone that is released in the body of a person who is feeling a strong emotion, such as excitement, fear, or anger, causing the heart to beat faster and giving the person a short-term boost in energy.

anger: A natural response to unexpected or disappointing circumstances. However, students who demonstrate consistent anger might be struggling with other feelings or emotions that should be addressed.

anxiety: A feeling of worry, nervousness, or unease, typically about an imminent event or something with an uncertain outcome. Although some anxiety is natural, excessive anxiety can impede learning.

collaboration: Working with others to share ideas or make something. Collaboration skills are expected to improve with maturity and self-awareness.

TEACHER TAKEAWAYS

- When students act angry or are uncooperative, it might be their way of masking other emotions or challenges. Try to break through and understand the root cause of the anger.

- Although a little anxiety can be a good thing, too much anxiety impedes learning. Working memory, attention, and processing speed are often most impacted by anxiety (Eysenck, Derakshan, Santos, & Calvo, 2007).

- One key source of anxiety is when there is a mismatch between expectations for a student (from teachers, parents, or the student) and the student's abilities and achievement.

- Health management can play an important role in helping students manage anxiety and stress. Promoting healthy habits such as a good night's sleep, eating a balanced meal, and getting daily exercise can help.

- Collaboration is an important life skill. Give students opportunities to work in groups and manage the challenges, perhaps without a grade attached. Learning to work with students who have different styles and habits is important. Consider grouping students with different cognitive strengths and needs so they begin to appreciate that everyone thinks differently and how different approaches can be equally successful. Sometimes combining approaches results in the best outcomes.

 ## STUDENT TAKEAWAYS

- Everyone feels anxious at times. Classmates who say they don't care or aren't nervous might very well be feeling anxious but do not want to admit it. You are not alone in feeling anxious or stressed.

- Anger and anxiety can interfere with learning. Certain strategies will help, some as easy as using a stress ball. Share your concerns with a trusted adult who can help you find the best supports.

- One major source of anxiety is fear, whether it is fear of the unknown or fear of making a mistake. Although it can be scary, the best way to overcome this type of anxiety is to jump in and try the task. The more you practice, the better you get and the less anxious you will be. Avoiding the task is only likely to make you more anxious.

- Many students do not enjoy group projects. Differing personalities and concerns about grades are just two of the reasons. However, group work is exactly the type of challenge you will face in the "real world." Learning how to find common goals and interests and giving everyone the opportunity to actively participate will minimize conflicts and maximize performance.

MINDPRINT STRATEGIES FOR STUDENTS

- Self-Empathy (*https://my.mindprintlearning.com/toolbox/toolbox-demo/product/12528*) (T, S)

- Strategies to Reduce Anxiety (*https://my.mindprintlearning.com/toolbox/toolbox-demo/search?name=&academic_topics=&cognitive_skills=2&interests=&product_types=3.10.11.12.13&age_range_min=3&age_range_max=21&order_by=bestfit_score+desc&uses_recommendations=&pills=cognitive_skills%7C2.&page=1*) (T, S)

- Strategies to Develop Collaboration Skills (*https://my.mindprintlearning.com/toolbox/toolbox-demo/search?name=&academic_topics=510&cognitive_skills=&interests=&product_types=10.3.11.12.13&age_range_min=3&age_range_max=21&order_by=bestfit_score+desc&uses_recommendations=&pills=academic_topics%7C510.&page=1*) (T, S)

A CLOSER LOOK

- Games, Websites and Apps for Group Work; Mindprint Learning (*https://my.mindprintlearning.com/toolbox/toolbox-demo/search?name=&academic_topics=510&cognitive_skills=&interests=135&product_types=1.2.4.5.6.7.8.9&age_range_min=3&age_range_max=21&order_by=bestfit_score+desc&uses_recommendations=&pills=interests%7C135.academic_topics%7C510*)

- Wellness Apps; Mindprint Learning (*https://my.mindprintlearning.com/toolbox/toolbox-demo/search?name=wellness&academic_topics=&cognitive_skills=&interests=.123&product_types=5.7.8.9&age_range_min=3&age_range_max=21&order_by=bestfit_score+desc&uses_recommendations=&pills=.interests%7C123*)

- What Causes Mindblanks During Exams? The Edvocate (*www.theedadvocate.org/causes-mind-blanks-exams/*)

LESSON ACTIVITIES

Direct Instruction

Understanding Personal Skills: Discuss the importance of personal skills. Use Figures 15-17. (E, M, H)

Teacher Background

All students, even those with the strongest academic performance, need to come to class ready to learn. Introduce the importance of personal skills in learning. Understanding strengths and difficulties in this area is as important for life success as understanding academic and cognitive skills.

Teacher-led Discussion

Personal skills include how we collaborate (cooperate) and communicate (listening, social language) with others. It also includes how we feel (happy, sad, comfortable, anxious), how we approach work (mindset), how we make decisions, and our character traits. Give examples of each skill as you go through them. Encourage examples from students.

In the context of academic learning, the personal skills that tend to have the most impact on performance are growth mindset, anger, anxiety, and collaboration.

We are going to spend some time thinking about our feelings and what makes us anxious or frustrated.

What is anxiety?

How can some anxiety help our performance (adrenaline)?

How can anxiety interfere with our learning?

What are things we can do to help work through anxiety or frustration? Make a list with the class. What have you tried? What has helped? What have adults suggested? Refer to Mindprint Learning strategies to reduce anxiety (*https://my.mindprintlearning.com/toolbox/uid/search?name=&academic_topics=&cognitive_skills=.2&interests=&product_types=3.10.11.12.13&age_range_min=3&age_range_max=21&order_by=bestfit_score+desc&uses_recommendations=&pills=.cognitive_skills%7C2*).

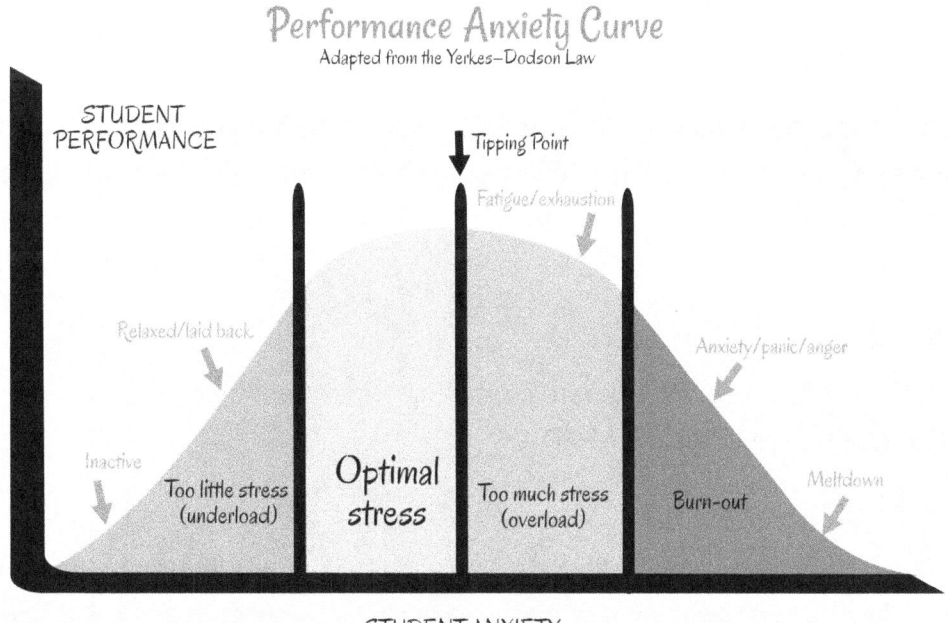

Figure 16: Performance anxiety curve

Share the Performance Anxiety graphic and explain the negative effects of anxiety and stress (Yerkes & Dodson, 1908). Although some level of stress is good to keep our minds energized and active, especially in time-sensitive situations like a test, too much stress can interfere with the mind's ability to think clearly and can impede performance. Discuss the importance of exercise, enough sleep, and good eating habits in reducing stress.

Student Activity

Throw Away Test Anxiety (*https://my.mindprintlearning.com/toolbox/toolbox-demo/product/1997*): Have students write their fears before a big test and "throw them away." (E, M, H)

Student Activity

Collaboration Skills (*https://my.mindprintlearning.com/toolbox/toolbox-demo/search?name=&academic_topics=510&cognitive_skills=&interests=&product_types=12&age_range_min=3&age_range_max=21&order_by=bestfit_score+desc&uses_recommendations=&pills=academic_topics%7C510.&page=2*): Using the Mindprint Learning website, ask students to print out and read the Group Work strategy for their strongest and weakest skills. Add strategies to their Personalized Learning Plans or folders. (M, H)

Student Activity

Group Reflection: After a group project, have students individually reflect on the group's performance. Have the students fill out the sheet independently, perhaps at home. If appropriate, have the group reconvene and discuss their reflections. (E, M, H)

Coaching

Mental Health Breaks: Incorporate stretching, movement, and mindfulness into daily classroom routines. (E, M, H)

Coaching

Student Groupings: Take a deliberate approach to your student groupings. Consider when you want to group students with similar strengths or similar needs. At other times, consider grouping students with dissimilar skills so they grow to appreciate the strengths and needs of others.

STUDENT ACTIVITY:
Group Reflection

Name: _____

Reflect on what went well in your group and what you wish had gone better. Do not use other students' names in your reflection.

What was your favorite part of working in this group?

Do you think this group exceeded the performance of what you could have done independently? Why or why not?

What are specific areas where this group could have done better?

If you were the group's coach or leader, what would you suggest they do differently on the next project?

Lesson 9

Nonacademic Skills: Cognitive

Cognitive skills drive your learning efficiency. They are the skills your brain uses to understand, solve problems, remember, plan, and pay attention. These skills, working together, determine how you most efficiently take in information and how you apply it in different situations such as writing, making a video, or taking a test. If you are having difficulty with one or more of these skills and are unaware of it, it could affect successful learning in one subject or across all classes.

Cognitive skills explain why you might learn some things easily whereas other tasks require more effort. They might explain why students who seem to understand in class have difficulty completing homework or doing well on a test. No one is equally strong in every cognitive skill. Understanding relative strengths and needs can go a long way in improving self-awareness and helping students minimize obstacles to learn more efficiently and enjoyably. Insight into cognitive skills often provides the key to unlocking students' innate talents and intrinsic interests.

It is important for educators and students to understand that you don't practice and study to improve cognitive skills. In this way, they are different from academic and even personal skills. Instead, you develop and use strategies to support cognitive skills over years so that you become more self-aware and, as a result, a stronger and more consistent learner by employing coping skills and effective learning strategies.

 **VITAL VOCAB**

cognitive skills: Skills that explain how you learn. These are very different from academic skills that identify what you know or have mastered. The four key domains of cognitive skills are complex reasoning, executive functions, memory, and speed.

complex reasoning: The higher-order reasoning skills that determine how you understand information. They include verbal reasoning (understanding what you read or hear), abstract reasoning (making sense of numbers, objects, or patterns), and spatial perception (understanding how objects relate in space).

executive functions: The cognitive skills needed for focusing, organizing your work and belongings, managing your time, and planning and following through on tasks. Includes attention, working memory, and flexible thinking.

memory: The skills used to store or remember information and retrieve it later when needed, including verbal memory (words) and visual memory (pictures, objects, or places).

speed: The rate at which you absorb, understand, and respond to information you hear, read, or see. Includes visual motor and processing (auditory and visual).

 TEACHER TAKEAWAYS

- Every student has a unique combination of cognitive strengths and needs.

- Most cognitive strengths and needs are not easily observable. Sometimes strengths mask needs, and vice versa. Students are unlikely to understand or communicate their difficulties with these skills unless they have received formal instruction or coaching.

- Cognitive strengths and needs are not necessarily predictors of academic achievement. However, if you understand a student's strengths and needs, you can use specific strategies to support a student who is struggling or a student who needs more of a challenge. Whether you set up a free Mindprint account or choose Comprehensive Mindprint, you can search and save favorite strategies in your Mindprint Toolbox.

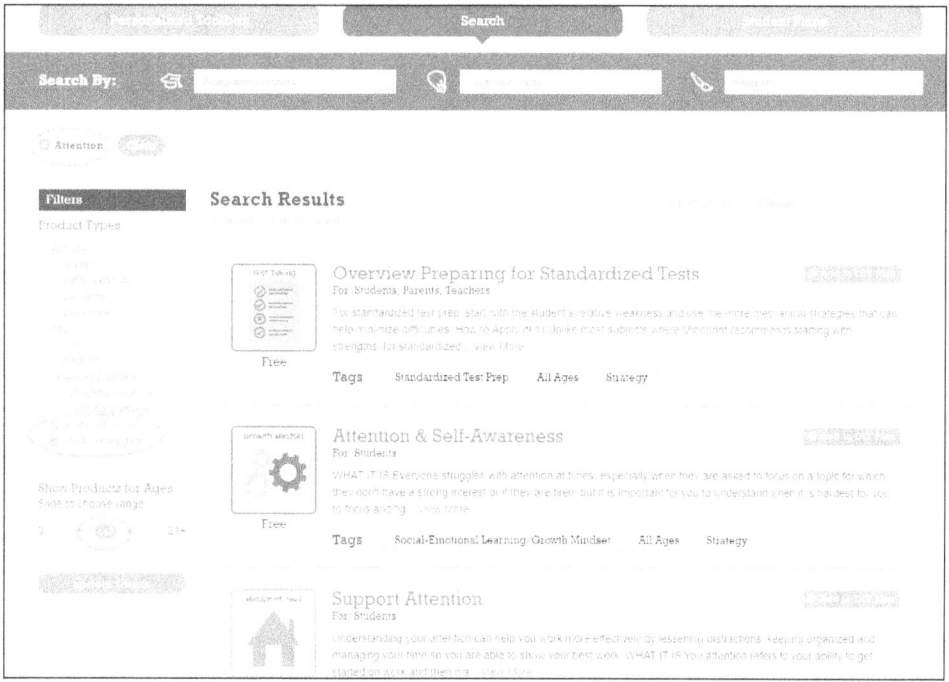

Figure 17: Custom search for cognitive skills

STUDENT TAKEAWAYS

☐ Everyone has relative strengths and needs.

☐ You can use your awareness of your cognitive skills to help you learn more easily. You are likely to discover that the study strategies that work best for your friend are not the right ones for you, and vice versa. The key to learning is using the right strategies *for you* when you need them.

☐ Once you discover your strengths, use them to make work easier and more enjoyable. They also might influence your choice of college major or career.

Overview of Cognitive Skills

SKILL	WHAT IT IS	WHEN YOU USE IT
Visual Motor Speed	Using your eyes and hands at the same time to complete a task	Typing; playing video games; sports that depend on eye-hand coordination
Processing Speed	Reading, hearing, or seeing information, thinking about it, and responding	Answering a question in class; finishing a test in the allotted time; taking the recommended time to complete a homework assignment
Attention	Focusing and completing a task, even if you don't like it	Listening carefully in class; completing homework without being frequently distracted
Working Memory	Juggling all the information you need to solve a problem or complete a task	Listening to your teacher while taking notes; packing up everything you need for school or home; following directions from your coach, teacher, or parent
Flexible Thinking	Taking feedback and adjusting	Figuring out how to correct your test or paper from what your teacher wrote; compromising after a disagreement with your friend or sibling; identifying multiple approaches to solve a problem

SKILL	WHAT IT IS	WHEN YOU USE IT
Verbal Reasoning	Understanding what you read or hear	Understanding themes of a book; understanding class discussion; picking up on nuances in a text or conversation
Abstract Reasoning	Understanding patterns, puzzles, or other non-language-based information	Figuring things out by observing; understanding math and science concepts that you can't always see or touch such as gravity, atoms, or algebra
Spatial Perception	Visualizing objects and how they move, even if you can't touch them	Picturing how pieces of a puzzle would fit together even before you touch them; imagining how you would draw a picture to scale or build something; visualizing 3D objects without a model
Verbal Memory	Remembering what you heard or read	Remembering a conversation, someone's name, or the specific details of a book you read
Visual Memory	Remembering what you saw	Remembering the details (color, size, shape) of pictures you saw, objects you've held, or places you've been

MINDPRINT STRATEGIES FOR STUDENTS

- Mindprint Skill Overview (*https://my.mindprintlearning.com/toolbox/toolbox-demo/search?name=&academic_topics=&cognitive_skills=&interests=&product_types=12&age_range_min=3&age_range_max=21&order_by=bestfit_score+desc&uses_recommendations=&pills=*) to explain and develop each cognitive skill (S, T)

- Strengths/Needs in Visual Motor Speed (*https://my.mindprintlearning.com/toolbox/toolbox-demo/search?name=&academic_topics=&cognitive_skills=44&interests=&product_types=12&age_range_min=3&age_range_max=21&order_by=bestfit_score+desc&uses_recommendations=&pills=cognitive_skills%7C44*)

- Strength/Needs in Processing Speed (*https://my.mindprintlearning.com/toolbox/toolbox-demo/search?name=&academic_topics=&cognitive_skills=41&interests=&product_types=12&age_range_min=3&age_range_max=21&order_by=bestfit_score+desc&uses_recommendations=&pills=cognitive_skills%7C41*)

- Strengths/Needs in Attention (*https://my.mindprintlearning.com/toolbox/toolbox-demo/search?name=&academic_topics=&cognitive_skills=30&interests=&product_types=12&age_range_min=3&age_range_max=21&order_by=bestfit_score+desc&uses_recommendations=&pills=cognitive_skills%7C30*)

- Strengths/Needs in Working Memory (*https://my.mindprintlearning.com/toolbox/toolbox-demo/search?name=&academic_topics=&cognitive_skills=23&interests=&product_types=12&age_range_min=3&age_range_max=21&order_by=bestfit_score+desc&uses_recommendations=&pills=cognitive_skills%7C23*)

- Strengths/Needs in Flexible Thinking (*https://my.mindprintlearning.com/toolbox/toolbox-demo/search?name=&academic_topics=&cognitive_skills=6&interests=&product_types=12&age_range_min=3&age_range_max=21&order_by=bestfit_score+desc&uses_recommendations=&pills=cognitive_skills%7C6*)

- Strengths/Needs in Abstract Reasoning (*https://my.mindprintlearning.com/toolbox/toolbox-demo/search?name=&academic_topics=&cognitive_skills=37&interests=&product_types=12&age_range_min=3&age_range_max=21&order_by=bestfit_score+desc&uses_recommendations=&pills=cognitive_skills%7C37*)

- Strengths/Needs in Verbal Reasoning (*https://my.mindprintlearning.com/toolbox/toolbox-demo/search?name=&academic_topics=&cognitive_skills=32&interests=&product_types=12&age_range_min=3&age_range_max=21&order_by=bestfit_score+desc&uses_recommendations=&pills=cognitive_skills%7C32*)

- Strengths/Needs in Spatial Perception (*https://my.mindprintlearning.com/toolbox/toolbox-demo/search?name=&academic_topics=&cognitive_skills=45&interests=&product_types=12&age_range_min=3&age_range_max=21&order_by=bestfit_score+desc&uses_recommendations=&pills=cognitive_skills%7C45*)

- Strengths/Needs in Verbal Memory (*https://my.mindprintlearning.com/toolbox/uid/search?name=&academic_topics=&cognitive_skills=34&interests=&product_types=12&age_range_min=3&age_range_max=21&order_by=bestfit_score+desc&uses_recommendations=&pills=cognitive_skills%7C34*)

- Strengths/Needs in Visual Memory (*https://my.mindprintlearning.com/toolbox/toolbox-demo/search?name=&academic_topics=&cognitive_skills=42&interests=&product_types=12&age_range_min=3&age_range_max=21&order_by=bestfit_score+desc&uses_recommendations=&pills=cognitive_skills%7C42*)

A CLOSER LOOK

- Articles on Cognitive Ability and Testing; Mindprint Learning (*https://mindprintlearning.com/article/topics/academic-potential/cognitive-ability-iq-testing*)

- Mindprint Observation Checklist: Identifying Learning Struggles; Mindprint Learning (*https://s3.amazonaws.com/wordpress_uploads/site/uploads/2014/04/Learning-Struggles-Checklist.pdf*)

- Understanding Learner Diversity; Mindprint Learning (*https://mindprintlearning.com/expert-advice/ability/uneven-performance/*)

LESSON ACTIVITIES

Direct Instruction

Cognitive Skills (E, M, H)

Teacher Background

Most students (and adults) do not have a good understanding of their cognitive skills. It will be important to help students build a basic understanding of them and their role in learning. Students should understand that everyone has a unique combination of cognitive strengths and needs. The key to successful long-term learning is to use your awareness of your cognitive skills to choose the learning strategies that enable you to succeed most easily.

Teacher-led Discussion

Refer back to the Sweet Spot of Learning Success (Figure 11). Explain that academic skills refer to what you know, whereas cognitive skills explain *how* you learn—including how quickly you work, remember information, solve problems, make decisions, organize, and focus. Cognitive skills might explain why you do not understand a particular concept and help us determine what we can try differently so you do understand.

Introduce the 10 core cognitive skills and give examples of how they use those skills in learning, in the classroom, during homework, etc. The Overview of Cognitive Skills offers full definitions and examples for your reference. Encourage students to give their own examples if they think of them. Consider making a poster for each skill so that students can view each skill and examples side by side. Let students know you don't expect them to learn or memorize these definitions—they will grow familiar with these skills as they learn about themselves through these exercises.

Student Activity

Personalized Learning Plan: Have students read the Mindprint overview on their strongest skills and those that need support:

https://my.mindprintlearning.com/search?name=&academic_topics=&cognitive_skills=&interests=&product_types=12&age_range_min=3&age_range_max=21&order_by=bestfit_score+desc&uses_recommendations=&pills=

For students who have a Mindprint Personalized Toolbox, add at least one strategy to their Personalized Learning Plan. (M, H)

Student Activity

How I Use My... worksheets: Have students complete one for a strength and one for a need. (E, M)

Student Activity

Cognitive Skills Prioritization: For students who have not taken the Mindprint Assessment and do not have a Mindprint Learner Profile, print out the 10 cognitive skills cards (found on the CAST Professional Publishing website at *http://castpublishing.org/books-media/empowered-student/resources/#lesson-9*). Have them self-assess and prioritize the skills from their strongest to those that need the most support. Encourage students to jot down notes or examples of why they picked specific skills as strengths or needs. (M, H)

Coaching

Teacher-led conferences for students who do not have a Mindprint Learner Profile: Meet with them individually to discuss their prioritization of their 10 cognitive skills. Keep in mind that most students will need support for this self-awareness exercise. The goal is to be directionally accurate so that each student feels confident in at least one strength and has at least one skill that you can agree where there is room for improvement. Consider using the Mindprint Observation Checklist to help you support students in this exercise.

Coaching

Teacher-led conferences for students who have taken the Mindprint Assessment: Meet with them individually to discuss their Learner Profiles. The following are suggestions on how to present the information and talking points for reviewing their assessments. (E, M, H)

AGE RANGE	DESCRIPTION	HOW
8-11, some older struggling learners	Verbally discuss results	Write down the student's top two strengths and one or two areas for support to visually reinforce what you will say
11-13	Share the summary chart	Print out the summary green, blue, purple chart Do *not* include the footnotes with percentiles Allow the child sufficient time to read and digest the chart while you are sitting nearby ready to answer questions
13+, some younger gifted learners	Share the entire report	Allow students to read the report independently before meeting Encourage them to reflect while they read

Suggested Talking Points for Reviewing the Assessment

Discuss how each person learns differently, using a unique combination of cognitive strengths and needs.

It is your unique combination of skills that will tell you how you learn best and how to pinpoint the best strategies to make learning easier and more enjoyable.

Encourage but don't require students to speak first. In general, do your best to *let them talk while you listen*. Let them explain why they think this report does or does not describe them. Maybe the score reflects performance on an off day. Or maybe it's an opportunity for you to help improve their self-awareness. Maybe you have less-confident students who do not appreciate their strengths. Or maybe you have overconfident students and this can be a good way to talk about areas where there is room for improvement. Use the report as a starting point for discussion and self-awareness development, not as a report card of cognition.

Always start with stronger skills. Think of concrete examples of when the skill has played a role in the child's success in school, in social situations, or on a team. Print out the overviews of the student's strengths so they appreciate the importance of these skills.

Keep in mind that *skills in the expected range are good skills*. Although these might not be the student's "go-to" skills, these skills can provide a solid foundation for successful learning. Be sensitive that top-performing students might feel that all their skills should be strengths. This is *never* true. No one has all strengths.

Never tell students they are bad at a skill. Rather, describe it as a skill that might cause difficulties at times. Talk openly about where that skill becomes important in and outside of school and what strategies students can use to make learning easier. Be prepared with two or three strategies for each student to use. The student overviews are a great place to start.

If a child is reluctant to discuss the results, *don't push*. Although an open and honest discussion is important, consider when it is appropriate to postpone part of the discussion for another day.

Consider *openly discussing your own strengths and needs*. This will further emphasize to the student that everyone has areas of strength and room for improvement. Talk about how you use your strengths and times when you struggled. Consider sharing stories of how you overcame some of your challenges and accomplished a goal.

STUDENT ACTIVITY:
How I Use My Visual Motor Speed

Visual Motor Speed Definition

Using your eyes and hands at the same time to complete a task

Examples:

Typing; playing video games; sports that depend on eye-hand coordination

Name: _____

I use my visual motor speed when I...

(Draw a picture, a short comic strip, or paste a photograph of yourself using this skill. Explain what it is and why the skill is important.)

STUDENT ACTIVITY:
How I Use My Processing Speed

Processing Speed Definition

Reading, hearing or seeing information, thinking about it, and responding

Examples:

Answering a question in class; finishing a test in the allotted time; taking the recommended time to complete a homework assignment

Name: _____

I use my processing speed when I…

(Draw a picture, a short comic strip, or paste a photograph of yourself using this skill. Explain what it is and why the skill is important.)

STUDENT ACTIVITY:
How I Use My Attention

Attention Definition

Focusing and completing a task, even if you don't like it

Examples:

Listening carefully in class; completing homework without being frequently distracted

Name: _____

I use my attention when I...

(Draw a picture, a short comic strip, or paste a photograph of yourself using this skill. Explain what it is and why the skill is important.)

STUDENT ACTIVITY:
How I Use My Working Memory

Working Memory Definition

Juggling all the information you need to solve a problem or complete a task

Examples:

Listening to your teacher while taking notes; packing up everything you need for school or home; following directions from your coach, teacher, or parent

Name: _____

I use my working memory when I...

(Draw a picture, a short comic strip, or paste a photograph of yourself using this skill. Explain what it is and why the skill is important.)

STUDENT ACTIVITY:
How I Use My Flexible Thinking

Flexible Thinking Definition

Taking feedback and changing your approach, even if you believe your first effort was good.

Examples:

Correcting your test or paper based on teacher comments; compromising after a disagreement with your friend or sibling; identifying multiple solutions or options for a challenging problem

Name: _____

I use my flexible thinking when I...

(Draw a picture, a short comic strip, or paste a photograph of yourself using this skill. Explain what it is and why the skill is important.)

STUDENT ACTIVITY:
How I Use My Verbal Reasoning

Verbal Reasoning Definition

Understanding what you read and hear

Examples:

Understanding themes of a book; understanding class discussion; picking up on nuances in a text or conversation

Name: _____

I use my verbal reasoning when I...

(Draw a picture, a short comic strip, or paste a photograph of yourself using this skill. Explain what it is and why the skill is important.)

STUDENT ACTIVITY:
How I Use My Abstract Reasoning

Abstract Reasoning Definition

Understanding patterns, puzzles, or other non-language-based information

Examples:

Figuring things out by observing; understanding math and science concepts that you can't always see or touch such as gravity, atoms, or algebra

Name: _____

I use my abstract reasoning when I...

(Draw a picture, a short comic strip, or paste a photograph of yourself using this skill. Explain what it is and why the skill is important.)

STUDENT ACTIVITY:
How I Use My Spatial Perception

Spatial Perception Definition

Visualizing objects and how they move, even if you can't touch them

Examples:

Picturing how pieces of a puzzle would fit together even before you touch them; imagining how you would draw a picture to scale or build something; visualizing 3D objects without a model

Name: _____

I use my spatial perception when I...

(Draw a picture, a short comic strip, or paste a photograph of yourself using this skill. Explain what it is and why the skill is important.)

STUDENT ACTIVITY:
How I Use My Verbal Memory

Verbal Memory Definition

Remembering what you heard or read

Examples:

Remembering a conversation, someone's name, or the specific details of a book you read

Name: _____

I use my verbal memory when I…

(Draw a picture, a short comic strip, or paste a photograph of yourself using this skill. Explain what it is and why the skill is important.)

STUDENT ACTIVITY:
How I Use My Visual Memory

Visual Memory Definition

Remembering what you saw

Examples:

Remembering the details (color, size, shape) of pictures you saw, objects you've held, or places you've been

Name: _____

I use my visual memory when I...

(Draw a picture, a short comic strip, or paste a photograph of yourself using this skill. Explain what it is and why the skill is important.)

PART 2

Three-Step Process to Self-Regulated Learning

With a strong foundation of metacognition, your students are prepared to drive their own learning. The following lessons will take you through the process of teaching students to set meaningful goals, choose strategies they will need to succeed, and monitor and adapt their approach as necessary. Although each student's goals and approach to learning will be different, you can use this structure to support all students.

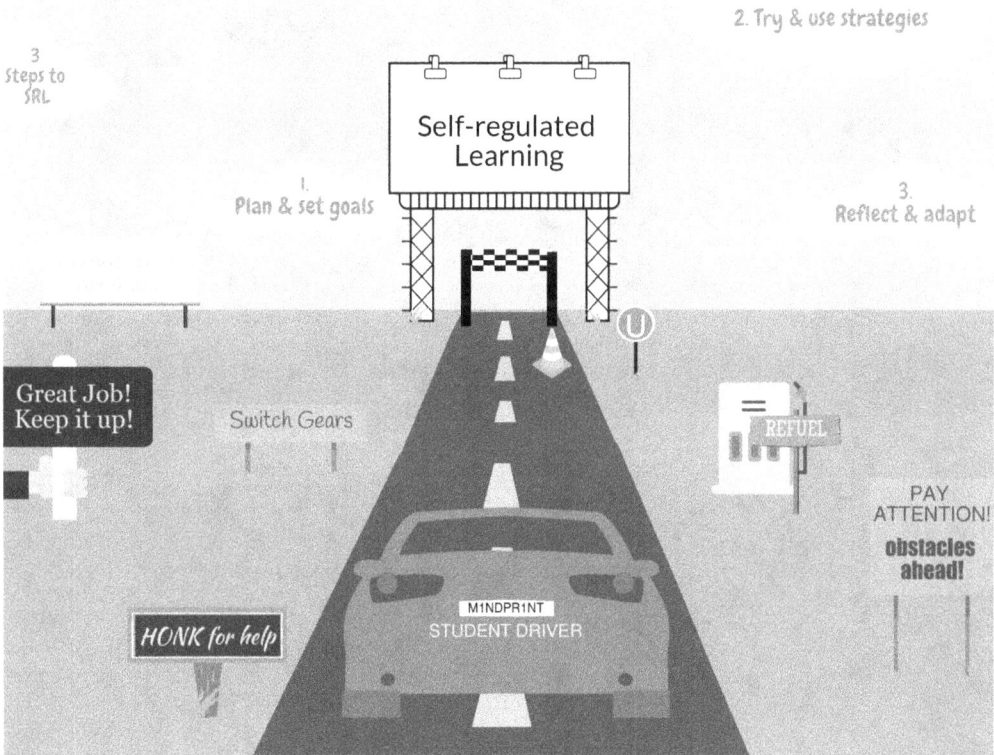

Figure 18: Students drive learning

Lesson Focus:
Step 1: Plan & Set Goals

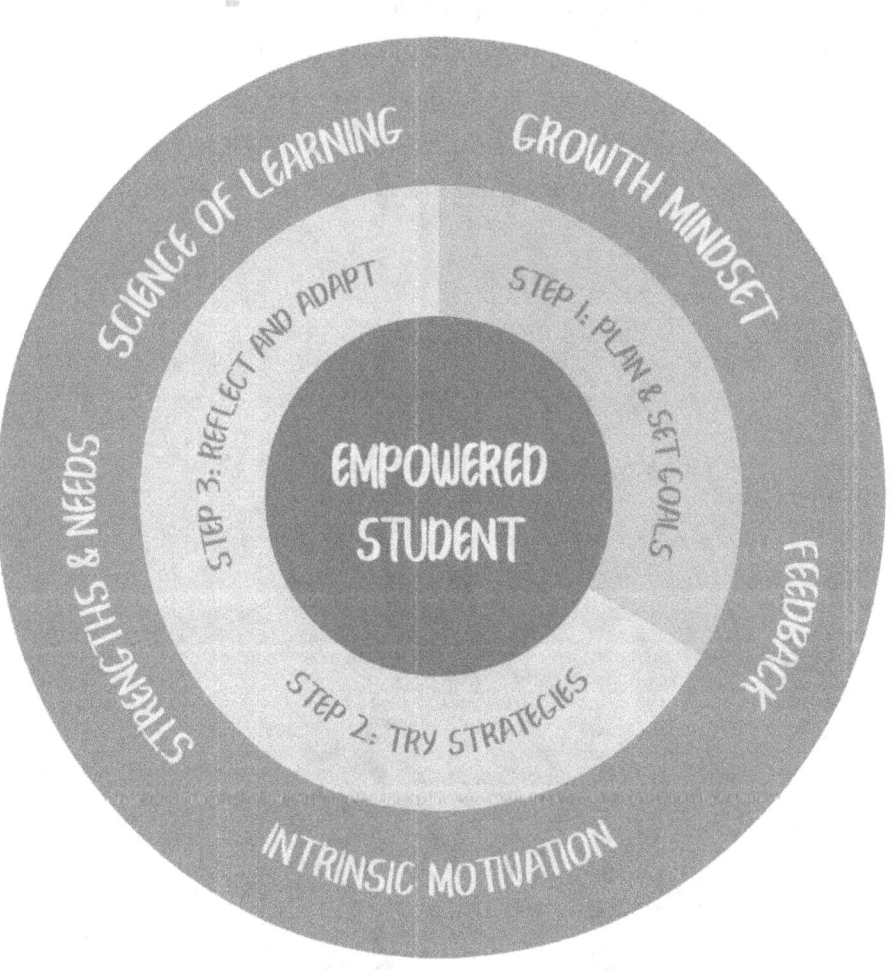

Figure 19: Plan & set goals

Lesson 10

Plan & Set Goals

Now that the students have identified their strengths and needs, they are well on their way to self-regulated learning. The next step is to help them make a personalized action plan that will place them in the driver's seat of their own learning. This plan includes setting specific goals to connect their capabilities to what they want to achieve in a manageable and realistic way.

TEACHER TAKEAWAYS

- ☐ Goals should be SMART (specific, measurable, achievable, relevant, and time-bound) (Doran, 1981).

- ☐ Goals should include a specific time frame (a week, a month, a marking period).

- ☐ Goals should include an objective method or measure to determine whether the goal was met at the end of the time frame.

- ☐ Goals should be a stretch but achievable. This is known as the zone of proximal development, or the "Goldilocks Principle." Are these goals achievable based on the student's strengths and needs? Are they too easy so the student won't grow? Are they too challenging and the student could easily be discouraged?

- ☐ Goals should reflect the student's intrinsic interests and should take into consideration academic, cognitive, and personal strengths and needs.

- ☐ Keep in mind that you want students to improve in all areas. Nurturing a strength could be as important as developing a weaker skill. Improving a social skill could be as important as improving a grade.

- ☐ Effective goal setting is dependent on self-awareness, planning, and flexible thinking. Goal setting might be harder for students with weaker executive functions (attention, working memory, or flexible thinking), but all students can be successful with support.

- ☐ Limit the number of goals. Too many goals can be unmanageable. The "Rule of Three" is a reliable benchmark. In some cases, one or two goals might be sufficient, especially for struggling learners or those with weaker executive functions

 ## STUDENT TAKEAWAYS

- ☐ The best way to achieve what you want in school (and in life) is to have a manageable plan of action by setting goals for yourself. If you are intentional about what you want to achieve, you are far more likely to succeed.

- ☐ Your goals can extend beyond grades or making the sports team. Think more broadly about the person you want to be.

- ☐ Plans and goals aren't permanent. They depend on what is going on in your life at a specific point in time and what is important to you. Identify what is important now. You can adapt your plans later as necessary.

 MINDPRINT STRATEGIES FOR STUDENTS

- Specific, Achievable Goals (*https://my.mindprintlearning.com/toolbox/toolbox-demo/product/1987*) (S)

- Discover True Interests (*https://my.mindprintlearning.com/toolbox/toolbox-demo/product/12530*) (S)

A CLOSER LOOK

- Articles on Interests & Passion; Mindprint Learning (*https://mindprintlearning.com/article/topics/academic-potential/interests-passion*)

- Student Interest Survey for Career Clusters; Advance CTE (*https://careertech.org/student-interest-survey*)

- SMART Goal Setting with Your Students; Edutopia (*www.edutopia.org/blog/smart-goal-setting-with-students-maurice-elias*)

LESSON ACTIVITIES

Direct Instruction

Teachers introduce the importance of goal setting.

Teacher Background

Students should have specific goals that reflect their Learner Profiles or student-prioritized cognitive skills. Unlike class goals such as getting an A or learning specific content, these goals should be about broader self-improvement and lifelong learning skills.

Teacher-led Discussion

Begin at the end—why are we doing this? Remind students that the ultimate objective is for them to take control of the learning process but that you will be there to support them along the way. Generate enthusiasm for the idea that they will be in control, not someone else telling them what they must do. Reinforce that the process is only successful if they take responsibility.

Show students the Self-Regulated Learning Overview (Figure 2). Take this opportunity to review the strong foundational skills they have been developing on the inside of the circle: establishing growth mindset, understanding their intrinsic motivations, and identifying their areas of strength and need in academics, cognitive, and personal skills.

Review the Three-Step Process they will take to develop self-regulated learning.

Emphasize the importance of goals being specific to students' own unique combination of strengths, needs, and interests. Acknowledge that this can be challenging at first but that it will get easier over time.

Provide reassurance that goals can and most likely will evolve. This is a fluid process—adjustments are expected.

Student Activity

Goals We Can Measure: This is a warm-up exercise that provides practice turning non-measurable goals into measurable goals. (E, M)

Direct Instruction/Student Activity

Individual Goal Setting: This is the most detailed and time-consuming exercise in this guide. Allow for sufficient preparation and time. (E, M, H)

Direct Instruction/Student Activity

Individual Goal Setting (Alternative Version) (*https://mindprintlearning.com/free-resources/mindprint-exclusives/*): You can download an Excel Goal Setting Spreadsheet as an alternative, self-guided approach to the three-step process. (M, H)

Coaching

Make Goals Visible: Place the goals in an accessible, visible spot—on your student binder or in a special folder, or hang them in the classroom. (E, M, H)

STUDENT ACTIVITY:
Goals We Can Measure

Before individual goal setting, have students think about how to write goals that can be measured. This can be done in small groups or as a class discussion. Begin with an example and then offer a series of goals that cannot be measured. Ask students to reword the goals to make them measurable:

PROMPTS	MAKE IT MEASURABLE	HOW I WILL MEASURE
I will do better in Math		
I will get organized		
I will work faster		

STUDENT ACTIVITY:
Individual Goal Setting

Name: _____

Keeping in mind my strengths and needs:

	MY STRONGEST SKILL	**SKILLS I NEED HELP WITH...**
Academic Skills		
Cognitive Skills		
Personal Skills		

What do I want to achieve in _____ over the next _____?
                                            (subject)   (time period)

Step 1: Brainstorm (At least _____ goals)

BRAINSTORM IDEAS	WHY IS THIS GOAL IMPORTANT TO ME?

Step 2: Are My Goals Realistic and Specific?

Look at your list and evaluate:

- Is the goal specific?
- Is the goal realistic?
- Can you accomplish the goal in the time frame?
- Is the goal written in the "positive"? (what you want to do, not what you don't want to do)
- Is the goal meaningful?

Rewrite your goals to make them positive, realistic, and specific in the given time frame. If there are goals that you can't make realistic or that really aren't important to you, you can leave them off the list.

REALISTIC AND SPECIFIC GOALS	TIME FRAME

Step 3: How will I decide if I achieved my goal? How will I measure if I am successful?

For each goal, decide on an objective measure.

REALISTIC & SPECIFIC GOALS	TIME FRAME	HOW WILL I MEASURE MY PERFORMANCE?

Step 4: Prioritize your goals.

Number your goals above in order of importance to you. Give a "1" to the goal you want to work on the most.

Step 5: My Goals!

Write your final goal(s) and how you will measure them below. Aim for three final goals.

MY GOALS	TIME FRAME TO COMPLETE	GOAL MEASURES

Lesson Focus:
Step 2: Try & Use Strategies

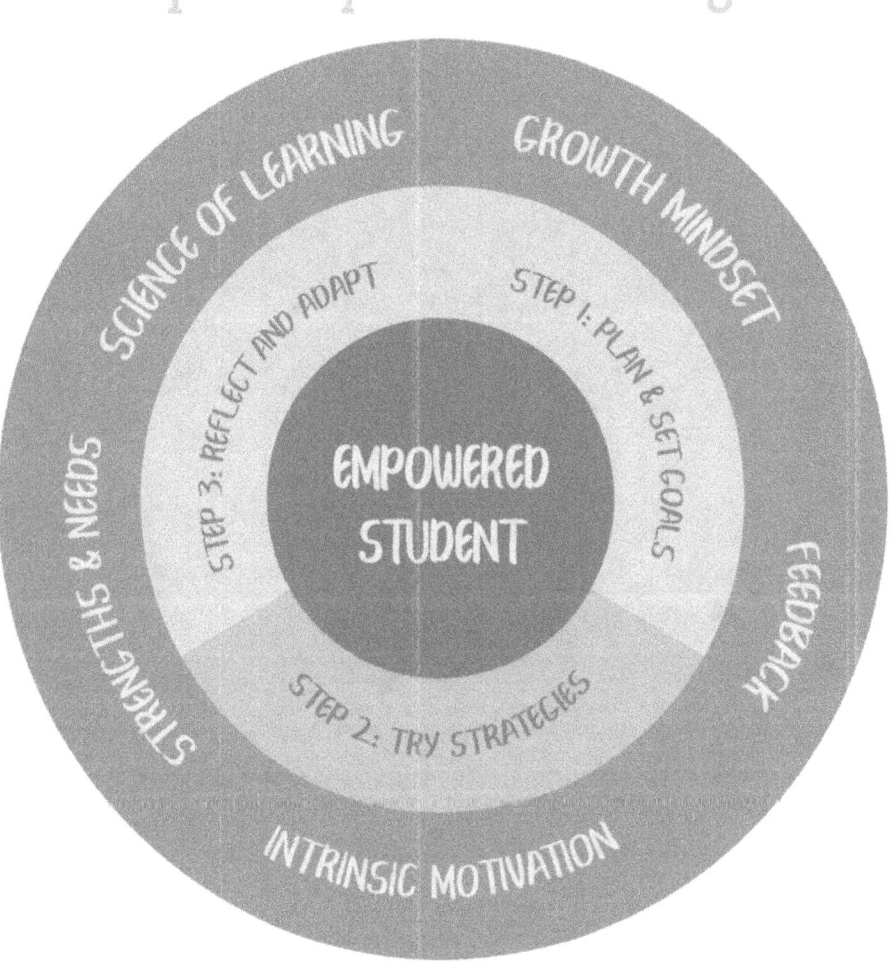

Figure 20: Try & use strategies

Lesson 11

Try & Use Strategies

Next students will select the specific strategies that will help them reach their goals. You will find that the Personalized Toolbox will enable students to easily narrow down their options based on their goals (e.g., class participation, getting organized), strengths, and needs. Ideally, students will include study strategies for homework time as well as strategies to use during class. Students without a Mindprint Learner Profile can still access all the same strategies for free, but they might need adult guidance to make good choices.

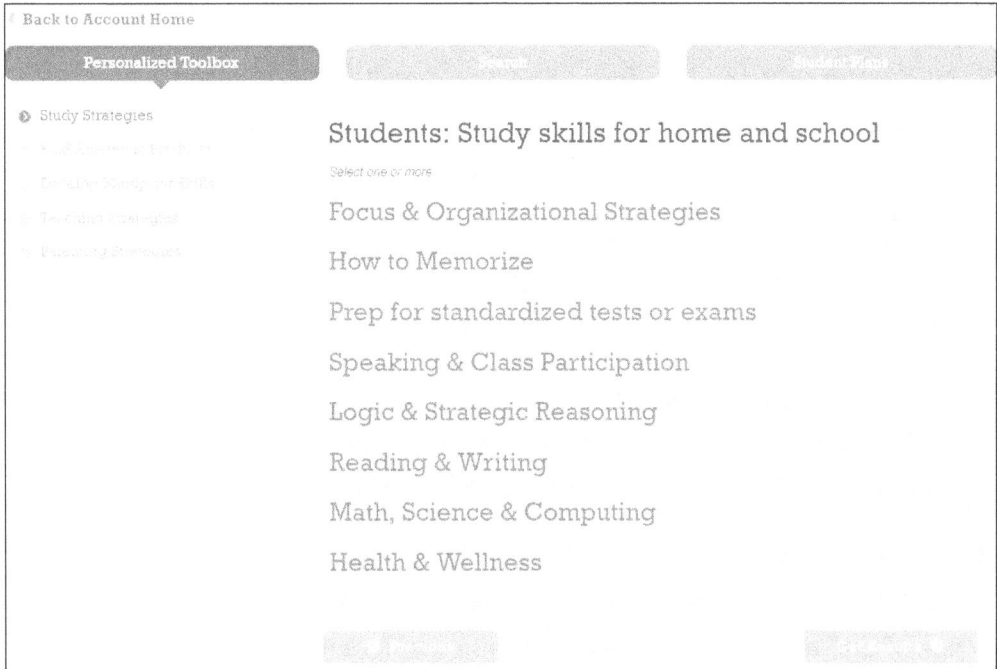

Figure 21: Personalized Toolbox

Using new strategies often requires changing old habits. Students might need support from teachers or parents, ranging from gentle reminders to more formal instruction. Consider which students are likely to know when to ask for help, and which students you might want to proactively support.

VITAL VOCAB

parenting strategies: Approaches parents can use to help students with homework or other academic, cognitive, or personal tasks.

study skills: Approaches that students take to improve their performance at home and in the classroom.

teaching strategies: Evidence-based supports that teachers use with students to cultivate strengths and support areas of need.

TEACHER TAKEAWAYS

- ☐ All strategies in the Mindprint Toolbox are evidenced based and effective. You will want to focus on helping students try strategies that will be most practical and beneficial for them based on their current needs, goals, and environment.

- ☐ It is best to limit students to no more than three new strategies at a time to increase the likelihood that they will follow through and be successful.

- ☐ Teachers can play a critical role in narrowing down options, but it is important for the students to ultimately choose the final strategies. Student-driven choices will increase the likelihood of follow-through.

- ☐ You might want your class to focus on a specific area, such as group work, growth mindset, or health and wellness, and have groups of students try a specific strategy. Use the Search tab in the Teacher's Mindprint Toolbox to identify strategies.

- ☐ Some of the strategies will require teacher or parent support to get started. Consider whether you want to encourage strategy choices based on these factors.

STUDENT TAKEAWAYS

- ☐ The process of choosing and trying the strategies that will work best for you will require some trial and error. Don't expect strategies to be easy or work perfectly the first time.

- ☐ Start with two or three strategies you believe will work best for you. In deciding, consider what you've tried in the past, your after-school schedule, and so forth.

- ☐ You might need help getting started with some of these strategies. Just ask. Or you might decide to abandon one strategy and try another.

 MINDPRINT STRATEGIES FOR STUDENTS

- Give Limited Options (*https://my.mindprintlearning.com/toolbox/toolbox-demo/product/1100*) (T)

- Create Contingency Plans (*https://my.mindprintlearning.com/toolbox/toolbox-demo/product/10779*) (T, S)

- Homework Wrappers (General and by Cognitive Skill) (*https://my.mindprintlearning.com/toolbox/toolbox-demo/product/12327*) (T, S)

 A CLOSER LOOK

- Getting Started with the Mindprint Toolbox; Mindprint Learning (*https://s3.amazonaws.com/wordpress_uploads/site/uploads/2015/05/MindprintGettingstarted.pdf*)

LESSON ACTIVITIES

Direct Instruction

What are strategies? Discuss the importance of deliberate strategy selection but also a willingness to try different strategies if one isn't working as expected. (E, M, H)

Teacher Background

Start by highlighting where students are in the process of Plan & Set Goals—Try & Use Strategies—Reflect & Adapt. Guide them to choose the best-fit strategies to help them meet their goals.

Teacher-led Discussion

Strategies are simply approaches to help you work more efficiently and effectively. You are trying strategies all the time to help you learn and work, whether or not you are aware of it. Examples include:

Organizational strategies: writing assignments in your notebook, checking off assignments as you complete them, estimating time for each assignment before you start.

Study strategies: flashcards, having a parent quiz you, saying words out loud.

Explain the process of hand-picking strategies based on what they know about themselves as learners and the goals they set.

Encourage students to choose two or three strategies initially. Remind them that this process involves some trial and error, and they might need to try a few strategies before discovering what works best.

Anticipate that some of the strategies will be new to both you and students. Be prepared to teach strategies, and help students practice with you before working independently.

Expect to check in with students to ensure that they are using the strategy successfully and make any needed adjustments.

Direct Instruction/Student Activity

Strategy Selection: Guide students in identifying strategies using the Mindprint Personalized Toolbox. If you have specific areas where you want students to focus, you should instruct students on the search criteria to use. Alternatively, you can print a list of strategies for students to select from. (E, M, H)

Direct Instruction/Student Activity

Developing Metacognition: Students will see quotes for 10 key metacognitive questions they can use to improve their self-awareness and performance. Have students identify the questions that resonate the most and add the corresponding strategies to their Mindprint Learning Plans. They can use the strategies even if they do not have a Learner Profile or have not set their specific goals. (E, M, H)

Student Activity

Strategy Action Plan: After choosing strategies, students should have a written action plan and both you and the student should have a copy. Students can use the template provided, or you can support students in customizing an action plan that is best suited for the student's planning and organizational needs. (E, M, H)

Student Activity

I Haven't YET gives students a visual motivator once they have chosen their strategies. Students can keep these papers in their assignment binders or consider hanging one up on the wall for inspiration. (E)

Student Activity

Create a Contingency Plan provides students with low-stakes practice in handling disappointment and planning ahead. Though important for all students, it might be particularly beneficial for anxious students or those with weaker flexible thinking. (E, M, H)

Coaching

Assignment/homework wrappers (*https://my.mindprintlearning.com/toolbox/toolbox-demo/product/12327*)—Customize wrappers to include the chosen strategies. (E, M, H)

STUDENT ACTIVITY: Strategy Selection

Name: _____

1. Pick one goal from Step 5 of the Goal Setting Worksheet.

MY GOAL	MY GOAL MEASURES

2a. Look in your Mindprint Personalized Toolbox under "Study Strategies" to find what strategies might help you meet your goal. Feel free to identify your own strategies too.

2b. Students without a Personalized Toolbox, you can use the Search tab. Select a skill from the Cognitive Skills dropdown menu. On the left sidebar, adjust the age range and deselect all product types except Mindprint Skills and Study Skills.

3. Make a list of strategies you find in your Mindprint Toolbox that you think are interesting.

4. Choose up to three strategies you will use. If you have difficulty deciding, use the template below to help you think through which strategies will be best.

STRATEGY	HOW WILL IT HELP ME?	WHEN WILL I USE IT?

STUDENT ACTIVITY: Strategy Action Plan

My Goal: _____

My Goal Measures: _____

STRATEGIES I WILL USE TO REACH MY GOAL	WHERE I NEED HELP/OTHER COMMENTS

Teacher Comments: _____

My Strategy Use: _____

	STRATEGY 1	STRATEGY 2	STRATEGY 3
Monday			
Tuesday			
Wednesday			
Thursday			
Friday			
Weekend			

STUDENT ACTIVITY:
I Haven't YET

Name: _____

I haven't

_____

_____

_____

YET...

But if I _____

_____

_____

I will be able to!

STUDENT ACTIVITY:
Developing Metacognition

Use these questions to help students think about their learning process. Encourage students to pick the three strategies they will find most useful, read about them, and add them to their Mindprint Learning Plan or Mindprint folder.

"Do I understand better when I read or when I see a picture or diagram? Will combining pictures or visuals with words help?"

- Draw Pictures of Word Problems (*https://my.mindprintlearning.com/toolbox/toolbox-demo/product/1917*)
- Visualization or Mind Movies (*https://my.mindprintlearning.com/toolbox/toolbox-demo/product/11520*)

"Do I fully understand the topic? How can I be sure?"

- "W" Questions to Encourage Deeper Analysis (*https://my.mindprintlearning.com/toolbox/toolbox-demo/product/10179*)
- Ask Questions (*https://my.mindprintlearning.com/toolbox/toolbox-demo/product/1944*)

"How can I apply what I already know to help me learn this subject more easily?"

- Make Connections to Previously Learned Information (Elaboration) (*https://my.mindprintlearning.com/toolbox/toolbox-demo/product/12302*)
- Activate Prior Knowledge (*https://my.mindprintlearning.com/toolbox/toolbox-demo/product/1900*)
- Diagramming Similarities and Differences (Analogical Reasoning) (*https://my.mindprintlearning.com/toolbox/toolbox-demo/product/11493*)

"Do I learn better when I work with someone else? How can I learn best when I study with my classmates?"

- Peer Teaching (*https://my.mindprintlearning.com/toolbox/toolbox-demo/product/12100*)
- Study Groups (*https://my.mindprintlearning.com/toolbox/toolbox-demo/product/11175*)
- Convince a Skeptic (*https://my.mindprintlearning.com/toolbox/toolbox-demo/product/11769*)

"Do I often cram and then sometimes forget on the test?"

- Spaced Repetition (*https://my.mindprintlearning.com/toolbox/toolbox-demo/product/11427*)

- Mix Up Content to Improve Learning & Retention (Interleaved Practice) (*https://my.mindprintlearning.com/toolbox/toolbox-demo/product/11511*)

"After I think I've finished studying, how will I be sure that I really know it?"
- Restate/Stop & Summarize (*https://my.mindprintlearning.com/toolbox/toolbox-demo/product/11507*)
- Use the Images in Non-fiction (*https://my.mindprintlearning.com/toolbox/toolbox-demo/product/11796*)
- Re-read & Re-write Notes (*https://my.mindprintlearning.com/toolbox/toolbox-demo/product/1294*)

"What do I do when I get 'stuck'?"
- Read Problem to an Adult (*https://my.mindprintlearning.com/toolbox/toolbox-demo/product/1836*)
- Restate/Stop & Summarize (*https://my.mindprintlearning.com/toolbox/toolbox-demo/product/11507*)

"How will I keep track of what I don't understand so I can get help later?"
- Save Questions (*https://my.mindprintlearning.com/toolbox/toolbox-demo/product/11488*)
- Prep for Teacher Review Sessions (*https://my.mindprintlearning.com/toolbox/toolbox-demo/product/11322*)

"How will I plan ahead for long-term projects or bigger assignments to make sure I'm not scrambling at the end?"
- Daily Reflection (*https://my.mindprintlearning.com/toolbox/toolbox-demo/product/10325*)
- Lists to Check Work (*https://my.mindprintlearning.com/toolbox/toolbox-demo/product/1726*)
- Self-Assess What You Know (*https://my.mindprintlearning.com/toolbox/toolbox-demo/product/11912*)

"Before I get started, do I have everything I need to be successful? How can I avoid realizing I forgot something at the last minute?"
- Homework Routine (*https://my.mindprintlearning.com/toolbox/toolbox-demo/product/1187*)
- Develop a System (*https://my.mindprintlearning.com/toolbox/toolbox-demo/product/12229*)
- Project Outline (*https://my.mindprintlearning.com/toolbox/toolbox-demo/product/1189*)

STUDENT ACTIVITY:
Create a Contingency Plan

Name: _____

One strategy to increase your likelihood of success is to anticipate what could go wrong and be prepared with a backup plan. Think about an important project, sporting event, or activity you have coming up. You want to be sure it is a success. How will you plan for the unexpected?

What is the event?

_____

List one or two things that could go wrong.

_____

_____

How will I prepare for the "just in case"? _____

_____

_____

Lesson Focus:
Step 3: Reflect & Adapt

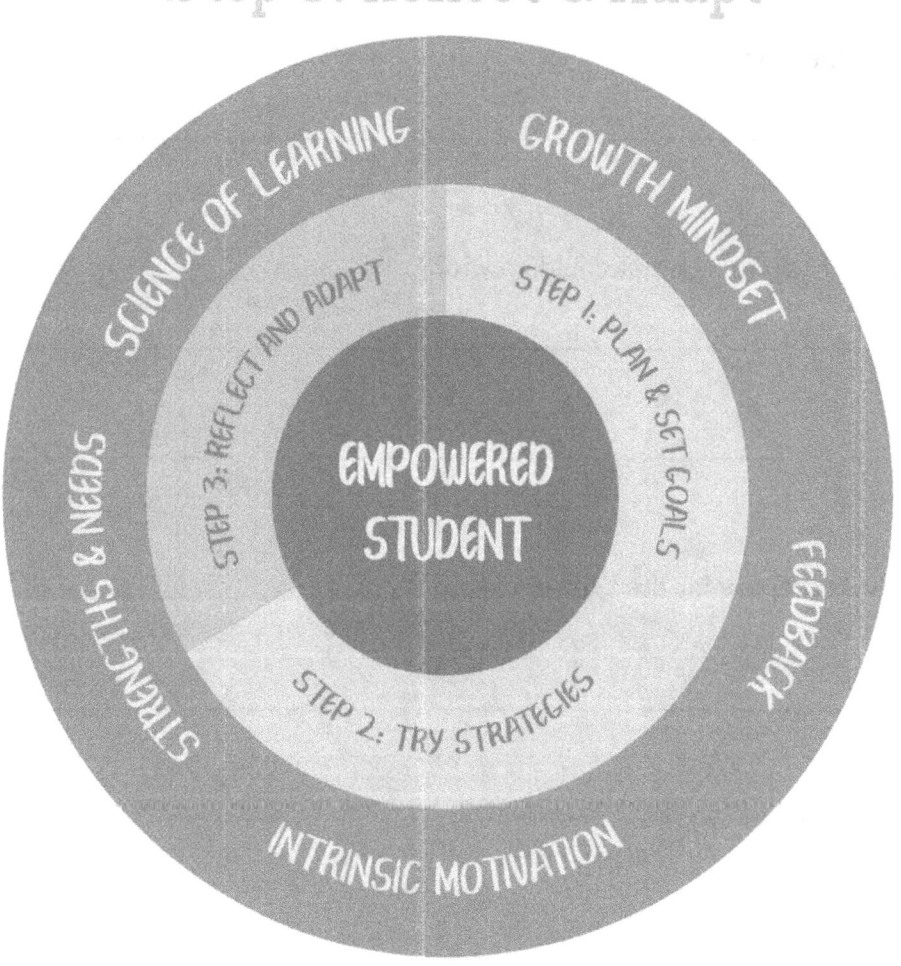

Figure 22: Reflect & adapt

Lesson 12

Reflect & Adapt

Students should expect to adjust their approach along the way in response to unanticipated events or challenges. Reflecting on performance and adapting is a critical aspect of self-regulated learning.

The frequency of deliberate reflection opportunities should depend on the time frame and importance of the goal. If students are working on longer-term goals, you do not want to let most of the term pass before realizing that goals will not be met. For a semester-long goal, plan for a minimum of two formal check-ins, one toward the beginning and another mid-semester. Since the ultimate objective is self-regulated learning, you will want to remind students to do self-check-ins on a more regular basis to ensure they are on track. Let them know you are available if they need help. If goals are short-term, maybe only a week or two, it might be fine not to have formal check-ins. Still, students should be reminded to do their own daily self-check-ins.

You will want to help students manage expectations around successes and what they might deem as failures in the goal-setting process. Be certain students understand that achieving goals sometimes takes longer than expected and sometimes they will not be successful even with extra time. Setting goals and striving for them is critical to self-improvement and growth. Encourage students to focus more on the incremental progress and process as opposed to the result. If success is unlikely, shift the focus to what students learned in the process and what they can do differently the next time. Most successful people will acknowledge that they learned more from their failures than they ever did from their successes.

VITAL VOCAB

adapting: Adjusting to circumstances based on feedback.

self-monitoring: Measuring, reflecting, and adjusting your behavior, thoughts, and feelings.

self-reflecting: Being introspective and willing to learn more about yourself to improve. Self-reflection should take into consideration performance based on academic, personal, and cognitive strengths and needs.

TEACHER TAKEAWAYS

- Students should be evaluating their efforts as well as their outcomes. Self-reflection on both measures is essential to instilling a growth mindset.

- Though accurate self-reflection and self-regulation are the ultimate goals, many students will need your help to decide what is working and what needs adjusting and how. There will be times when it is best to support students before they fail, and times when it will be important for them to learn from their own mistakes.

- Some students might need more hands-on coaching in how to take feedback, reflect on it, and adapt. Anticipate that students with weaker flexible thinking will need extra support.

STUDENT TAKEAWAYS

☐ Don't be discouraged if you don't meet all your goals with the first strategies you tried. Expect for your plan to evolve. It's typical to need to try several different strategies before you find the ones that are most effective for you.

☐ One of the most important skills you can develop is a willingness to take feedback from your teacher, peers, or parents and adjust mid-course. Your ability to grow and improve is just as important as, if not more important than, meeting the goal.

☐ Be honest with yourself. If you have a hard time taking feedback, try not to respond immediately when someone gives you feedback. Try to just listen before you decide to incorporate the feedback. Ultimately, you are responsible for your actions and the changes you make.

 MINDPRINT STRATEGIES FOR STUDENTS

- Daily Reflection (*https://my.mindprintlearning.com/toolbox/toolbox-demo/product/10325*) (S)

- Homework Wrapper (*https://my.mindprintlearning.com/toolbox/toolbox-demo/product/12327*) (S, T)

- Balanced, Specific Feedback (*https://my.mindprintlearning.com/toolbox/toolbox-demo/product/11503*) (T)

- Coach How to Take Feedback (*https://my.mindprintlearning.com/toolbox/toolbox-demo/product/12262*) (T)

- Prompt Feedback (*https://my.mindprintlearning.com/toolbox/toolbox-demo/product/1901*) (T)

A CLOSER LOOK

- Articles on Flexible Thinking; Mindprint Learning (*https://mindprintlearning.com/article/topics/executive-functions/21st-century-skills-flexible-thinking*)

- *The Explosive Child*, by Ross Greene (*https://my.mindprintlearning.com/toolbox/toolbox-demo/product/12073*)

- The Developing Engagement with Feedback Toolkit; Higher Education Academy (*www.heacademy.ac.uk/system/files/resources/the_developing_engagement_with_feedback_toolkit_deft_0.pdf*)

- 7 Reflection Tips for Assessment, Empowerment, and Self-Awareness; Edutopia (*www.edutopia.org/blog/reflection-assessment-empowerment-self-awareness-james-kobialka*)

LESSON ACTIVITIES

Direct Instruction

Let's Talk about Reflection: What is reflection and why does it help? (E, M, H)

Teacher Background

Introduce the importance of self-reflection through a class discussion. Help students appreciate that reflection is open-ended and there is no one right way to approach it.

Teacher-led Discussion

Start the discussion with open-ended questions: *What is reflection? What are we doing when we reflect?*

It might help to have the students jot down a few words on a paper and then share them with the class to make a mind map on the board. Answers might include: *reviewing your work, thinking about what you did*, and *thinking about why you did it.*

Ask, why do we reflect?

Again, make a map with students' answers. Answers might include:

So we can get better

So we can remember what we did

So we can decide what to do differently

So we know what to do next

So we can think about a mistake

Connect this brainstorm to how students will be reflecting on their use of strategies and how the strategies are helping them achieve their goals.

Remind students that reflecting and adapting is a key part of the learning process. *You need to think about what you are doing to know/decide whether or not it is working. You will likely need to try several different strategies before finding the best ones to reach your goals, and that takes reflection and shifting.*

Student Activity

Assignment Wrappers: You can provide students with a "wrapper" or checklist of ideas to think about before an assignment so students are most likely to use the best strategy for the specific assignment (Eberly Center, Carnegie Mellon University, 2016). After students complete the assignment, they are asked to reflect on whether they used the strategies and whether they were helpful. The included assignment wrapper is an example to guide you. You can create specific wrappers based on each student's strengths and needs or use more generalized wrappers for the class based on the academic subject. Alternatively, you can have students create their own wrappers using the strategies they chose in the previous lesson. To make the wrappers manageable, typically a list of three to five items is best. (E, M, H)

Student Activity

Interim Reflection: This worksheet can be filled out by students to reflect on their goal progress and use of their chosen strategies. Then they can meet with a peer of their choice to discuss. Students can use this worksheet for each of their goals. Be sure students have had sufficient time to learn and apply the strategies. (E, M, H)

Student Activity

Track Progress: If a strategy needs to be used regularly to be effective, create a way to track it. For example, if the goal is to participate in class three times per week, print a calendar and check it off each day. (E, M, H)

Coaching

Daily Reflection: Encourage students to take 5 or 10 minutes at the end of class or at home before bedtime a few times a week to quietly self-reflect. This can be written or more informal think time. (E, M, H)

Coaching

Model Reflection: Share out loud thoughts on a lesson or discussion on what you might do differently next time. Reflection could be related to time management, class participation, or connection of information to previous topics. (E, M, H)

Coaching

Shout-outs: Allow for student "shout-outs" at the end of class where students call out something positive that a classmate did that day. Add that to a shout-out wall to encourage positivity and a supportive environment. (E, M, H)

Coaching

Ongoing use of assignment wrappers. (E, M, H)

STUDENT ACTIVITY:
Assignment Wrapper (example)

FRONT PAGE

Name: _____

While reading I can...

- ☐ Think about how the topic/material connects to what I already know or we are learning in class.

- ☐ Make a mental picture (mind movie) of what I am reading.

- ☐ Highlight main ideas, details, and key vocabulary words.

- ☐ Stop and summarize to myself the main idea after reading each paragraph.

- ☐ Write down questions as I go so I can go back later or ask in class tomorrow.

When I finish, I can...

- ☐ Summarize the key takeaways in a few bullets.

If I'm having difficulty, I can...

- ☐ Read text aloud to myself or an adult.

- ☐ Use visual note-taking or draw a visual timeline to help me understand the sequence of events and facts.

- ☐ Look at the pictures and diagrams in the text for clues.

REFLECT & ADAPT

BACK PAGE

While reading, I...

- ☐ Thought about how the topic/material connected to what I already know or we are learning in class.
- ☐ Made a mental picture (mind movie) of what I am reading.
- ☐ Highlighted main ideas, details, and key vocabulary words.
- ☐ Stopped and summarized to myself the main idea after reading each paragraph.
- ☐ Wrote down questions and went back to them and/or will ask tomorrow in class.
- ☐ Summarized the key takeaways in a few bullets after I finished.

When I wasn't certain, I...

- ☐ Read text aloud to myself or an adult.
- ☐ Used visual note-taking or drew a visual timeline to help me understand sequence of events and facts.
- ☐ Looked at the pictures and diagrams for clues.

Where do I need help?

_____

_____

Or

I'd like my teacher to know...

_____

_____

STUDENT ACTIVITY:
Interim Reflection

Name: _____

My goal was:

How I'm doing:

I met/am making good progress to meet my goal.

I am making progress toward my goal, but there's a chance I won't meet it.

I am unlikely to meet or am making insufficient progress toward my goal.

If you might not meet your goal, things to think about:

Was I able to focus the entire time? See attention strategies.

Did I have trouble following instructions or following through? See attention or working memory strategies.

Did I have trouble remembering what I needed? See memory strategies.

Did I have trouble finishing? See organization strategies.

Did I have trouble understanding? See critical thinking strategies.

Which of my strategies helped, and are there any I should adapt or abandon?

Strategy 1	
I used this strategy when…	
It helped me…	
It wasn't useful when…	
I will continue to use it, but adapt it by…	
I will not use this strategy but will find another one (write new strategy into your action plan).	
Strategy 2	
I used this strategy when…	
It helped me…	
It wasn't useful when…	
I will continue to use it, but adapt it by…	
I will not use this strategy but will find another one (write new strategy into your action plan).	

Strategy 3	
I used this strategy when…	
It helped me…	
It wasn't useful when…	
I will continue to use it, but adapt it by…	
I will not use this strategy but will find another one (write new strategy into your action plan).	

Conclusion

With the three-step framework, we provide an approach that can help all students become self-regulated learners in any environment or situation they encounter. However, we don't want you or them to expect it will be a straightforward and easy path. Developing self-regulation is hard work.

We encourage you to view this as a journey that will take students time to embrace and integrate into all aspects of their learning. You'll recall that the journey started with building critical foundational skills around understanding how their brain works and how progress is made through effort and a growth mindset. We focused on increasing students' self-awareness about their own unique combinations of strengths, needs, and intrinsic interests. We cannot overemphasize the importance of this strong foundation and allowing each student to spend as much time as she or he needs to build it. You might be surprised to discover which of your learners embrace this new approach and which struggle with this process of self-discovery and self-awareness.

Only when the foundational skills are in place can students really begin to take control of their learning. They can use their knowledge of how they learn best to make a specific plan of action that involves setting realistic goals and choosing and trying strategies that will help them reach those goals. Each student's plan will be unique because each student is unique. As students move ahead, they once again will need your help in an ongoing process of listening to feedback, reflecting, and adapting. Again, you might be surprised by which learners have the most difficulty accepting feedback and adopting a new approach.

Always remember that the road to self-regulated learning is open to all students. However, most will need supportive adults to ensure that they are always moving forward, even if they are moving slowly. The key will be understanding students' starting points and meeting them there, not where you might expect them to be. They are finding their best way and they need you to be their coach, cheerleader, and supporter. By continually reinforcing the concepts and activities covered in this book, you will be giving your students an invaluable gift—the gift of how they learn—and leading them to become more motivated, self-confident, and ultimately, successful.

References

CAST (2012, August 14). UDL and expert learners. Retrieved from *www.udlcenter.org/aboutudl/expertlearners*

CAST (2018). Universal Design for Learning Guidelines version 2.2. Wakefield, MA: Author.

Center on the Developing Child, Harvard University. (2012). Executive function (InBrief). Retrieved from *https://developingchild.harvard.edu/resources/inbrief-executive-function/*

Center on the Developing Child, Harvard University. (2017). Key concepts: Brain architecture. Retrieved from *https://developingchild.harvard.edu/science/key-concepts/brain-architecture/*

Doran, G. (1981). There's a S.M.A.R.T. way to write management's goals and objectives. *Management Review, 70*(11), 35–36.

Duckworth, A. (2016). *Grit: The power of passion and perseverance.* New York, NY: Scribner.

Dweck, C. S. (2016). *Mindset: The new psychology of success.* New York, NY: Random House.

Ebbinghaus, H. (2013). Memory: A contribution to experimental psychology. *Annals of neurosciences 20,* 155–156.

Eberly Center, Carnegie Mellon University (2016). Exam Wrappers. Retrieved from *https://www.cmu.edu/teaching/designteach/teach/examwrappers/*

Eysenck, M., Derakshan, N., Santos, R., & Calvo, M. (2007). Anxiety and cognitive performance: Attentional control theory. *Emotion, 7*(2), 336–353.

Gray, A. (2016, January 19). The 10 skills you need to thrive in the Fourth Industrial Revolution. World Economic Forum. Retrieved from *www.weforum.org/agenda/2016/01/the-10-skills-you-need-to-thrive-in-the-fourth-industrial-revolution/*

Harackiewicz, J., & Hulleman, C. (2010). The importance of interest: The role of achievement. *Social and Personality Psychology Compass, 4*(1), 42–52.

Higgins, S., Kokotsaki, D., & Coe, R. (2012, July). Teaching and learning toolkit. Education Endowment Foundation. Retrieved from *https://v1.educationendowmentfoundation.org.uk/uploads/pdf/Teaching_and_Learning_Toolkit_(July_12).pdf*

Kohn, A. (1993). *Punished by rewards: The trouble with gold stars, incentive plans, A's, praise, and other bribes.* New York, NY: Houghton, Mifflin, Harcourt Publishing Company.

Kruger, J., & Dunning, D. (1999). Unskilled and unaware of it: How difficulties in recognizing one's own incompetence lead to inflated self-assessments. *Journal of Personality and Social Psychology, 77*(6), 1121–1134.

Lawson, C. (2002, January 1). The connections between emotions and learning. The Center for Development & Learning. Retrieved from *www.cdl.org/articles/the-connections-between-emotions-and-learning/*

Meyer, A., Rose, D. H., & Gordon, D. (2014). *Universal Design for Learning: Theory and practice.* Wakefield, MA: CAST Professional Publishing.

Moore, T. M., Reise, S. P., Gur, R. E., Hakonarson, H., & Gur, R. C. (2015). Psychometric properties of the Penn Computerized Neurocognitive Battery. *Neuropsychology, 29*(2), 235–246.

Panadero, E. (2017). A review of self-regulated learning: Six models and four directions for research. *Frontiers in Psychology, 8,* 422. Retrieved from *http://doi.org/10.3389/fpsyg.2017.00422*

Passler, K., Beinicke, A., & Hell, B. (2015, May–June). Interests and intelligence: A meta-analysis. *Intelligence, 50,* 30–51.

Yerkes, R. M., & Dodson, J. D. (1908). The relation of strength of stimulus to rapidity of habit-formation. *Journal of Comparative Neurology and Psychology, 18,* 459–482.

Zimmerman, B., & Schunk, D. (1989). *Self-regulated learning and academic achievement: Theory, research, and practice.* New York, NY: Springer-Verlag.

www.ingramcontent.com/pod-product-compliance
Lightning Source LLC
Chambersburg PA
CBHW082029120526
44592CB00038B/2313